C000069395

IAN ALLAN

British Rail
Locomotives
and other motive power

combined volume 12/6

First published 1967
Reprinted 2022

ISBN 9781800351448

Printed in India by Replika Press Pvt. Ltd.

Published by Crécy Publishing Ltd
1a Ringway Trading Est, Shadowmoss Rd
Manchester M22 5LH

Visit the Crécy Publishing website at www.crecy.co.uk

Front cover:
An unidentified BRCW Type 3 (later Class 33) at Weymouth on 31 August 1967.
Rev A. M. Logan/Online Transport archive

Rear cover:
Seen at Clapham Junction on 23 July 1966 is No. E6029; when recorded here the
locomotive was virtually brand-new, having entered service three months earlier.
Rev. A. M. Logan/Online Transport Archive

abc
BRITISH RAILWAYS
LOCOMOTIVES
and
other motive power

LONDON

IAN ALLAN

12/6

Standard Class 9F 2-10-0 No. 92110 and Class 7P6F 4-6-2s Nos. 70022 *Tornado* and 70013 *Oliver Cromwell* at Crewe
[D. L. Percival]

CONTENTS

Cover picture: "Western class 2,700 h.p. C-C diesel-hydraulic locomotive No. D1062 *Western Courier* approaching Acock's Green, Birmingham, with the 15.10 Paddington–Wolverhampton on June 11, 1963."

[*M. Mensing*

The last outpost of steam on British Railways is in the North West of England between Manchester, Warrington, Liverpool and Carlisle. From the beginning of 1968 the Carlisle area lost its steam locomotives after which they worked no farther north than Carnforth. The "Britannia" Pacifics worked out their last days on passenger, freight and parcels trains between Crewe and Carlisle; No. 70011 Hotspur drifts down the Lune Valley with a Carlisle–Crewe freight on July 22, 1967.

[J. H. Cooper Smith

4

BRITISH RAILWAYS MOTIVE POWER SURVEY

W ITH the end of steam traction on British Railways in 1968 it is opportune to review current BR motive power practice, in particular the changes in operating techniques which have occurred over the last 10 years or so. It was in 1955 that British Railways launched its massive modernisation programme which envisaged new forms of traction, the elimination of steam, new electrification programmes, and resignalling with colour-light signals and centralised power signalboxes on a scale not seen before in this country. At that time steam was supreme, although diesel traction was already prominent in a few places. Indeed, the LMS had introduced diesel shunters in the early 1930s and the Great Western had developed diesel railcars for branch and cross-country services at about the same time. Electric traction, too, was not new; the first conversions to electric-working had taken place as long ago as 1903/4 in the Newcastle and Liverpool areas but generally speaking electrification in 1955 was confined to suburban lines around Tyneside, Merseyside and Manchester, and North West and East London, also the Southern network including the main lines to Brighton, Eastbourne, Hastings and Portsmouth. Of particular importance was the newly electrified Manchester–Sheffield main line, inaugurated in 1954.

The major electrification schemes of the 1955 Plan have naturally taken some years to complete. The massive London Midland main line electrification between Euston, Liverpool and Manchester was finished only a year ago and the final extensions of the Southern network to Bournemouth in July 1967, the remaining Southern main lines to Dover and Ramsgate having been electrified in 1959/62. Suburban electrification has also been extended in North East London and electrification appeared in Glasgow for the first time. This system was also completed during 1967 with the conversion of the lines to Gourock and Wemyss Bay. Other schemes were also proposed, as for example Kings Cross to York; although this plan was later postponed it has been resuscitated in modified form to cover outer suburban

The Stanier Class 5 4-6-0s are among the last steam classes to survive on BR. No. 45209 is seen drawing slowly away from Tebay on the climb to Shap summit. At the rear, the train is banked by Standard Class 4 4-6-0 No. 75037. The latter engines took over banking duties on the climb to Shap during 1967 but their reign was short-lived for Clayton Type 1 diesels took over these duties from January 1, 1968.   [Derek Cross

6

services from Kings Cross, although it has not yet received Government approval for work to start. More advanced are plans for extension of electrification between Crewe, Carlisle and Glasgow, although here, too, the scheme has not been officially authorised and work is not likely to start before 1970 at the earliest.

Electrification Systems

Three main systems of electrification are employed on British Railways, the low voltage d.c. system (600–750V), employing conductor rails with current collected by bogie mounted shoes; the high voltage d.c. system (1,500V) using overhead catenary with current collected through pantographs mounted on locomotive and coach roofs; and the much higher voltage a.c. system (6,250/25,000V), again using overhead catenary with current collection through pantographs. The low voltage d.c. system is used for the Southern electric network and also the original suburban electrifications in North West London, Merseyside and Tyneside. The London area electrification of the LMR between Euston, Watford, Broad Street and Richmond, in fact, uses a fourth rail for the traction return current instead of the running rails used elsewhere on BR with this system. One disadvantage of the low voltage d.c. system is that where high horse powers are required for rapid acceleration or for sustained high speeds with heavy trains, the current (amperage) drawn by trains nears the practical limit of the low voltage d.c. system. It will be remembered that by Ohms Law, for a given amount of work, the higher the voltage employed, the lower will be the current (amperage) drawn. It is amperage that determines the size of cables in the power supply. Thus the low voltage d.c. system, while using only 600/750V—only three times the voltage of domestic house mains—requires heavy cabling on feeder supplies and on trains to withstand very high currents. It is for this reason that main line electrification schemes have generally been carried out using much higher voltages with the overhead catenary system. The higher voltage demands greater insulation and is unsuited for conductor rail used near the ground. At first the standard main line British electrification voltage was 1,500V d.c., first seen in an electrification scheme of the North Eastern Railway commissioned in 1915 but later abandoned. This system was also used for the 1931 Manchester–Altrincham scheme and between Liverpool Street, Shenfield and Southend

On the LMR electrified lines from Euston electric locomotives handle most long-distance passenger, freight and parcels services. The Euston–Liverpool/Manchester expresses are composed of fairly standard formations, mostly made up of Mark II integral construction coaches such as those seen here behind Class AL6 locomotive No. E3134 photographed approaching Kilsby tunnel with the 15.00 Euston–Manchester on May 14, 1966.

J. H. Cooper Smith

(1949/56) and between Manchester and Sheffield (1954). There was also the 6,600V 25 cycle a.c. system using overhead catenary but this was confined to the Lancaster–Heysham line and to some South London suburban lines. The latter were converted to the d.c. third rail system in the mid 1920s.

At first BR decided to continue with the 1,500V d.c. electrification system but with the development in France of a.c. electrification at the industrial frequency of 50 cycles, the high voltage a.c. system was found to have considerable advantages and was adopted as the future standard on BR. Subsequently the Liverpool Street suburban lines were converted to this system.

With high voltage the current drawn by trains is very low; thus cables can be very light and, above all, the copper conductor wire of the catenary can be very much smaller in section than that needed for 1,500V d.c. Moreover, with the higher voltage, voltage drop, which occurs as the distance from substations increase, is very much less marked. The distance between sub-stations can be very much greater with the high voltage a.c. system than with low voltage d.c. In certain parts of the Southern electric area, for example, sub-stations are no more than two miles apart, but on the LMR Euston–Liverpool–Manchester line they are about 50 miles apart. But the reduced cost of the simpler catenary and power distribution network of the high voltage a.c. system is offset by an increase in the complexity of equipment on trains, since conventional direct current traction motors are normally used on BR a.c. trains; thus the train equipment must include a transformer to reduce the voltage and a rectifier to convert it from alternating to direct current. On a.c. electric multiple-units all this equipment is mounted on the carriage underframe on motor coaches. The actual design and layout of equipment on a.c. locomotives and motor coaches varies from type to type depending on the builder; moreover, modifications have been necessary as a result of experience since the introduction of the first a.c. trains.

High voltage a.c. electrification (LMR, ER, ScR)

For the first of the recent a.c. electrification schemes it was decided to employ dual voltage working; because the high voltage (25,000V) required a clearance of 11in above and below the catenary for insulation purposes many overbridges required lifting. On some sections of line, particularly near city centres,

Many of the Waterloo–Bournemouth expresses are now powered by four-car high horse power electric units classified as 4REP. They include two 1,600 h.p. motor coaches, which because of the high current are equipped with two collector shoes on each side of both bogies. Unit No. 3001 is seen here standing at Basingstoke.　　　[R. E. Ruffell]

this was impracticable or unjustifiably costly. For these in-town sections it was decided to use a lower voltage (6,250V) and to arrange the equipment on the train for working on either voltage. The clearance above and below the catenary with the lower voltage was only 4in which meant that many bridges did not need to be rebuilt to obtain the greater clearance for the higher voltage.

The change in operating voltage to the trains is achieved automatically. At the junction between the two voltages there is a dead section of catenary. On the approach side of the change-over point magnets placed on each side of the running rails attract equipment on the train as it passes over, which opens the train circuit breaker. The train then coasts through the dead section and as it reaches the next live section of different voltage, a voltage sensing device on the train detects the change in voltage and alters the transformer tappings to suit the new voltage. The train passes over a further set of magnets which re-set the circuit breaker and power is again applied to the equipment. Voltage changeover equipment is found on Great Eastern lines where most of the lines in the London area, including the South-end Central branch from Shenfield, are electrified at 6,250V. The voltage changeover point is situated just east of Shenfield on the main line. On the LT&SR lines between Fenchurch Street and Shoeburyness the lower voltage is used as far as Barking and again between Chalkwell and Shoeburyness. Similarly, in Glasgow the lower voltage is used in the inner Glasgow area, particularly on the underground sections.

On the LMR a.c. lines, however, although it was originally planned to use the lower voltage in the London area it was found that the 11in clearance above and below the catenary was over-generous and could be reduced to 8in. Thus it was possible to electrify the whole line between Euston, Liverpool and Manchester at 25,000V. The first 100 LMR electric locomotives were fitted with dual voltage equipment but the lower voltage connections are locked out of use.

On BR a.c. lines locomotives are used only on the LMR. On the GE and Scottish Region electrifications, multiple-units cover all passenger services within the electrified area, but diesel locomotives are employed for freight services and for long-distance passenger trains originating outside the electrified lines. On the LMR, multiple-units are used for local workings in the London, Birmingham, Liverpool and Manchester areas

The other coaches used on Bournemouth express services are formed into four-coach unpowered sets with driving cabs at each end, known as 4TC. They are normally worked in conjunction with 4REP units but can also be powered by an electro-diesel locomotive. One of these locomotives is seen here at the back of a down Bournemouth express passing Walton-on-Thames. The driver is controlling the locomotive from the leading coach. The 4TC sets are also capable of being powered by certain SR Type 3 diesel locomotives.

K. P. Lawrence

12

and electric locomotives for nearly all long-distance passenger, freight and parcels trains. Some local freight and parcels services are worked by diesel locomotives, particularly if shunting in non-electrified yards at intermediate stations is necessary. Some of the multiple-units, nevertheless, cover long distances and the outer suburban trains from Euston regularly run through to Birmingham. Indeed, some of the diagrams are arranged for the trains to continue onwards as a separate service through to Manchester.

Apart from the Southern Region, the use of d.c. electrification is now obsolete and in due course it seems likely that the remaining d.c. networks will disappear, either by being handed over to diesel traction or converted to the a.c. overhead system. Already the Newcastle area third rail system, one of the pioneer electrifications of 1903, has gone, its services being taken over by diesel multiple-units. The Manchester–Altrincham line, which operates at 1,500V d.c., makes an end-on junction with the Manchester area a.c. electrified lines and it seems likely that the former will be converted to a.c. to allow through running by a.c. trains.

One system which remains to be mentioned is the unique third rail system used on the Manchester–Bury line. Unlike normal third rail systems it employs side contact, in which the shoes carried on the train bogies press against the side of the conductor rail instead of on top as is normal practice. The conductor rail itself is protected on the outside by wooden boarding and a higher than normal voltage of 1,200V d.c. is used.

Southern d.c. electric units

The Southern Region d.c. network uses multiple-units for most of its services. SR multiple-units are broadly divided into three types for suburban, semi-fast and express services. Suburban trains are made up generally of non-corridor units with second class only accommodation. Semi-fast units usually have toilet facilities in part of the train and include first class accommodation, while trains for express duty have through gangways from coach to coach, toilet facilities, first and second class accommodation and, very often, refreshment facilities as well.

Because of detail differences it is not possible for all types of Southern multiple-unit to work together on the same train. The

Many diesel multiple-units of different make can be coupled together and controlled from the leading driving cab like this five-car train composed of four Metropolitan-Cammell cars with a Birmingham RCW Co. car at the front. The blue square coupling code can be clearly seen on each side of the yellow warning panel on the front of the car. The train is seen leaving Leeds for the Calder Valley line on March 17, 1967.

[L. A. Nixon]

main difference today lies in the type of braking. Since 1951 all new Southern electric units have been fitted with electro-pneumatic brakes, a development of the Westinghouse air brake which is applied and released electrically. Older types of stock built before this do not have the electro-pneumatic feature and, therefore, cannot run with EP fitted units in normal service. Moreover, the older type units have side buffers and screw couplings only, at the outer ends of the set, but the later units have buck-eye automatic couplers as well. In addition, while the older suburban (4SUB) and semi-fast (2BIL, 2HAL) units can work together they cannot work in multiple with the older express sets (4COR, 4BUF, 4GRI and 6COR). Although the older express sets can work with each other, the surviving 6COR units are now confined largely to the South Eastern Division and the 4COR, 4BUF and 4GRI units to the Waterloo–Portsmouth express service and to peak-hour services between Waterloo and Farnham and on the Central Division.

In contrast the more modern types of stock can work together and it is possible to see suburban, semi-fast and express units on the same train. These units normally include the letter P or EP in their classification, for example 4EPB, 2HAP, 4CEP, 4VEP, etc. The Brighton line express units are an exception since they include the letters IG (4CIG, 4BIG), the old LBSCR telegraphic code for Brighton. Otherwise SR classification letters indicate the type of accommodation the initial letter C denoting a corridor unit and B denoting buffet unit. The derivation of the classification 2HAP may not be obvious at first sight but can be traced back to the old Southern Railway codes of 2NOL, 2HAL and 2BIL (respectively, no lavatory, half lavatory and both lavatory, depending on whether toilet facilities were provided in either one or both coaches of a two-car set or not provided at all). The 2HAP provides similar accommodation to a 2HAL, but is fitted with electro-pneumatic brakes.

The 4VEP units on the South Western and Central Divisions combine suburban type layout with side doors to each seating bay or compartment, but with toilet and first class accommodation and through gangways. They are designed for long-distance stopping services, for example between Waterloo and Bournemouth, but have the facility that they may also be used with a conductor-guard if the Southern ever adopts ticket issue on trains on lightly used electric services in the future.

Diesel multiple-units on British Railways are allowed to take extra parcels vans at the back provided that the total weight does not exceed the limits of the power available. A three-car unit with an extra van is seen here near Dorchester on a Weymouth–Westbury working on May 18, 1966.

[C. W. R. Bowman]

Bournemouth express services introduced a form of operation new to BR main lines, for most trains operate on the push-pull principle. This is not new in itself, for two- or three-coach steam push-pull trains operated many branch or main line stopping services in the past; in Britain, however, we have never had long trains worked in this fashion, although they have been used in France, Germany and Switzerland for many years. On the Bournemouth line this is achieved by using unpowered four-car corridor units (4TC) fitted with driving cabs at each end. In the normal way power is provided by a four-car electric unit of special design with two 1,600 h.p. motor coaches (4REP). The 4REP units also include refreshment facilities. The reason for this form of operation lay in the fact that it was still considered desirable to provide through coaches to Weymouth, and the line from Bournemouth to Weymouth is not electrified; thus the through portions between Bournemouth and Weymouth are powered by diesel locomotives.

The Southern has adopted a control system in its latest multiple-units which allows different forms of traction to work in multiple. This is achieved by a 27-line control cable which provides all the controls necessary to work normal multiple-unit equipment, certain of the SR's Type 3 diesel locomotives and the small and large electro-diesels. Thus the 4TC units can be worked in conjunction with a 4REP unit or with a Type 3 diesel or with an electro-diesel, with the powered unit at either end or in between two 4TC units. The same simple controller in the 4TC driving cab is used whatever the motive power. Such is the flexibility of this system that it even allows different forms of traction to be used on the same train. Heavier trains may thus be powered by an electro-diesel and a Type 3 diesel, or either of these types of locomotive in combination with a normal electric multiple-unit, all controlled by one man in the leading cab. On the Southern's South Western Division it is possible, therefore, to see some trains powered by locomotives at the back, in the middle, in front, or in combinations with other locomotives and multiple-units. In normal service, however, the 4REP units cannot work in multiple with other powered units because of the high current which would be drawn which would tax the traction supply to the limit.

Freight and parcels services on the SR are normally handled by Type 3 diesels or electro-diesels. On the South Eastern Division, however, there are still 14 of the original 24 straight

On the East Coast main line "Deltic" Type 5 diesel locomotives handle the principal high-speed expresses. No. D9006 The Fife and Forfar Yeomanry heads the down "Tees-Tyne Pullman" through Hadley Wood on the northern outskirts of London. [Eric Treacy

electric locomotives, and the three original Southern Railway electric locomotives are still used on the Central Division. They were originally provided with pantographs for working in yards electrified with overhead conductor wires where third rails would be dangerous to shunters, etc. However, the Southern has now decided to use electro-diesels for this sort of work to save the cost of installation of overhead wires in yards. To this end the Region developed the electro-diesel locomotive which is a normal third rail electric locomotive but with a small diesel engine to provide low power when working over non-electrified lines. Some freight and a few passenger services on the Southern are powered by diesel locomotives from other regions, particularly the WR "Warships" between Waterloo and Exeter and on certain freight services on the Southampton line.

Diesel multiple-units

Elsewhere on British Railways diesel traction is supreme. Diesel multiple-units operate a large number of local, cross-country and main line services and, like SR electric units, are broadly divided into three types—suburban, semi-fast and express. Semi-fast units with toilet and first class accommodation are more general purpose in character, for the same unit can be found on branch line stopping services one day and on longer distance excursions the next, such is their flexibility in operation. Most diesel units are gangwayed within the set and a few are gangwayed right through the train. The majority of diesel multiple-units employ mechanical transmission, with a gearbox rather like a bus, but some have hydraulic torque-convertor transmission. Some units, those on the SR, for example, and the diesel Pullmans on the WR, use electric transmission in which the diesel engine drives an electric generator to provide current for electric traction motors.

The SR's local diesel electric multiple-units are very similar to the region's electric stock in appearance. Indeed, they are basically a diesel version of the 2HAP electric units, although most are made up into three-car sets. An exception is on the Hastings line where special six-car corridor and buffet units provide all services; these units are of special body design, no more than 8ft 2½in wide, to allow for the limited clearances between Tunbridge Wells and Hastings.

The Lickey Incline, one of Britain's steepest main line gradients—two miles at 1 in 37—on the Birmingham–Bristol main line, has always needed the service of banking engines to assist trains up the incline. Since dieselisation English Electric Type 3s have been employed, as for example No. D6938 seen at the rear of the 10.40 Bristol–Birmingham on July 21, 1964. However, these locomotives have since been transferred away from Bromsgrove and banking duties are now performed by WR Hymek Type 3s.

[Anthony A. Vickers]

Rapidly increasing in number on BR are Freightliner trains composed entirely of bogie flat wagons loaded with standard containers. They are air-braked and are not normally re-marshalled intermediately for they run throughout between starting and destination stations. Although the Freightliner, seen here behind Brush Type 4 diesel No. D1949, has a brake van for the guard next to the engine, these trains and other fully brake fitted freight and parcels trains do not need guards vans, for the guard now rides on the locomotive.

[Derek Cross

21

Diesel locomotives

Diesel locomotives on BR are of many styles and types. Most of those on the Western Region employ hydraulic transmission, but electric transmission is used elsewhere on main line locomotives. A few shunters have mechanical transmission with clutch and gearbox but this form of transmission is not suited to main line locomotives. At the start of dieselisation on British Railways many manufacturers supplied prototype classes but the standard locomotives evolved since then have come down in favour of the English Electric Type 1, the British Railways-built Type 2 with Sulzer engine, the English Electric Type 3 and the Brush 2,750 h.p. Type 4 with Sulzer engine, although English Electric are now in the course of delivering fifty 2,700 h.p. diesel-electric locomotives. The higher horse-power range over 3,000 b.h.p. is met by the twenty-two "Deltic" Type 5 locomotives on the East Coast main line; now, however, there are calls for diesel locomotives of even higher power. To this end Brush Traction have introduced a prototype 4,000 h.p. locomotive, No. HS4000 *Kestrel*, which will be tried out on BR to assess its performance. Whether we shall see bulk orders of this type in future years may depend on future electrification programmes.

Following withdrawal of a number of services and re-deployment of locomotives and multiple-units it has been decided to withdraw a number of non-standard diesel locomotives and multiple-units. Indeed, during 1967 over 250 diesel locomotives were withdrawn from service.

Unlike the days of steam where the larger express locomotives were normally confined to passenger work, diesel locomotives are mixed traffic in nature and except for the "Deltic" diesels on the East Coast main line, largely used on high-speed passenger services, all other classes may be found on passenger, freight and parcels trains. Several types can work in multiple, controlled by the driver in the cab of the leading locomotive; because of design differences not all types can work together. For this reason various types of locomotive and multiple-unit are grouped into classes that can work in multiple, which is denoted by coupling code symbols painted on the ends of each unit. The most common coupling code for diesel locomotives is a blue star, and in the case of diesel multiple-units a blue square. Only units bearing like symbols can work with each other. In the case of locomotives, those classes not given a symbol cannot work in multiple with any other class or even with other members of the same class. That does not mean to say that two locomotives cannot work together on the same train, but if they do each must have its own driver. Normally, multiple working is confined to Type 1, Type 2, Type 3 and some WR Type 4 locomotives.

On the steeply-graded South Devon main line of the WR between Newton Abbot and Plymouth, which includes stretches of 1 in 36, trains are normally double-headed rather than banked, with the assisting locomotive working right through. NBL Type 2 diesel No. D6312 and "Warship" Type 4 No. D868 *Zephyr* surmount the top of Dainton bank from Totnes with a Plymouth–Paddington train on August 19, 1961.   [M. Pope

BRITISH RAILWAYS LOCOMOTIVE
SHEDS AND SHED CODES
AND PRINCIPAL SIGNING-ON POINTS

All B.R. steam locomotives carry the code of their home depot on a small plate affixed to the smokebox door.

Diesel and electric locomotives carry the plate on the cab side or have the depot name painted on the buffer beam.

LONDON MIDLAND REGION

LMW	**Western A.C. Lines**	8A	**Edge Hill (Liverpool)**
		8C	Speke Junction
WL	**Western Lines**	8E	Northwich
		8F	Springs Branch (Wigan)
ML	**Midland Lines**	8H	Birkenhead
		8J	Allerton
DO1	**London (Western) Division**		
1A	**Willesden**		
1D	Marylebone		
1E	Bletchley	9A	**Longsight (Manchester)**
1F	Rugby	9B	Stockport (Edgeley)
1H	Northampton	9C	Reddish
		9D	Newton Heath
		9E	Trafford Park
DO2	**Birmingham Division**	9F	Heaton Mersey
		9H	Patricroft
		9K	Bolton
2A	**Tyseley**	9L	Buxton
2E	Saltley		
2F	Bescot		
DO5	**Stoke Division**	10A	**Carnforth**
		10D	Lostock Hall
		10E	Accrington
5A	**Crewe Diesel Depot**	10F	Rose Grove
5C	Stafford		
5D	Stoke & Cockshute		
6A	**Chester (Midland)**		
6C	Croes Newydd	12A	**Carlisle (Kingmoor)**
6D	Shrewsbury	12B	Carlisle (Upperby)
6F	Machynlleth	12C	Barrow
	Aberystwyth (V. of R.)	12D	Workington
6J	Holyhead	12E	Tebay

D14	**London (Midland) Division**	D16	**Nottingham Division**

14A	**Cricklewood East**
14C	Bedford

16A	**Toton**
	(Stapleford & Sandiacre)
16B	Colwick
16C	Derby
16D	Nottingham
16E	Kirkby-in-Ashfield
16F	Burton
16G	Westhouses

D15	**Leicester Division**

15A	**Leicester (Midland)**
	Market Harborough
15B	Wellingborough

EASTERN REGION

30A	**Stratford**

36A	**Doncaster**
36C	Frodingham

31A	**Cambridge**
31B	March

40A	**Lincoln**
40B	Immingham
40F	Boston

32A	**Norwich (Thorpe)**
32B	Ipswich

41A	**Tinsley (Sheffield)**
41C	Wath
41D	Canklow
41E	Staveley (Barrow Hill)
41J	Shirebrook West

34D	Hitchin
34E	New England
34G	Finsbury Park

NORTH EASTERN REGION

50B	Hull (Dairycoates)
	Hull (Alexandra Dock)
50C	Hull (Botanic Gardens)
50D	Goole

52G	Sunderland
52H	Tyne Dock
52K	Consett

51A	**Darlington**
51C	West Hartlepool
51L	Thornaby

55A	**Leeds (Holbeck)**
55B	York
55C	Healey Mills
55D	Royston
55E	Normanton
55F	Bradford (Hammerton St.)
	Keighley
55G	Knottingley
55H	Leeds (Neville Hill)

52A	**Gateshead**
	Bowes Bridge
52B	Heaton
52C	Blaydon
	Alston
52D	Tweedmouth

SCOTTISH REGION

60A	**Inverness (Lochgorm)**	**64A**	**St. Margarets (Edinburgh)**
	Forres		Galashiels
	Kyle of Lochalsh		Granton
60B	Aviemore		North Berwick
60D	Wick		South Leith
	Thurso	**64B**	Haymarket
			Millerhill
		64F	Bathgate
61A	**Kittybrewster**	**64G**	Hawick
	Inverurie	**64H**	Leith Central
61B	Aberdeen (Ferryhill)		
		65A	**Eastfield (Glasgow)**
		65B	St. Rollox
		65E	Kipps
		65F	Grangemouth
		65J	Stirling
62A	**Thornton**		
	Anstruther		
	Burntisland	**66A**	**Polmadie (Glasgow)**
	Kirkcaldy	**66B**	Motherwell
	Ladybank	**66C**	Hamilton
	Methil	**66D**	Greenock (Ladyburn)
62B	Dundee	**66E**	Carstairs
	Montrose	**66F**	Beattock
	St. Andrews		
62C	Dunfermline		
	Alloa		
63A	**Perth**	**67A**	**Corkerhill (Glasgow)**
63B	Fort William	**67B**	Hurlford
	Mallaig	**67C**	Ayr
63C	Oban	**67E**	Dumfries
	Ballachulish	**67F**	Stranraer

SOUTHERN REGION

70B	Feltham	**73F**	Chart Leacon
70D	Eastleigh		Ashford (Kent)
70F	Bournemouth		
70H	Ryde (I.O.W.)		
		75A	**Brighton**
73C	Hither Green	**75C**	Selhurst
73D	St. Leonards	**75D**	Stewarts Lane

WESTERN REGION

81A	**Old Oak Common**		84A	**Laira (Plymouth)**
81C	Southall		84B	St. Blazey
81D	Reading		84D	Penzance
81F	Oxford			

<table>
<tr><td>82A</td><td>Bristol (Bath Road)</td><td></td><td>85A</td><td>Worcester</td></tr>
<tr><td></td><td>Marsh Junction</td><td></td><td>85B</td><td>Gloucester (Horton Road)</td></tr>
<tr><td>82C</td><td>Swindon</td><td></td><td></td><td></td></tr>
<tr><td></td><td></td><td></td><td>86A</td><td>Canton (Cardiff)</td></tr>
<tr><td></td><td></td><td></td><td>86B</td><td>Newport (Ebbw Junction)</td></tr>
</table>

83A	**Newton Abbot**		87A	**Neath**
83B	Taunton		87B	Margam
83C	Westbury		87E	Landore

B.R. STEAM LOCOMOTIVES

THE following notes are a guide to the system of reference marks and other details given in the lists of dimensions shown for each class.

Many of the classes listed are sub-divided by reason of mechanical or constructional differences. At the head of each class will be found a list of such sub-divisions, if any, usually arranged in order of introduction. Each part is given there a reference mark by which its relevant dimensions, if differing from those of other parts, and the locomotives included in this sub-division, or part, may be identified. Any other differences between locomotives are also included, with reference marks, below the details of the class's introduction. The date on which the first locomotive of a class was built or modified is denoted by "Introduced."

The lists of dimensions at the head of each class show steam locomotives fitted with two inside cylinders, and slide valves, unless otherwise stated, e.g. (O) = two outside cylinders. All steam engines are superheated unless otherwise stated (NS= non-superheated).

The code shown in the headings to each class, e.g. "5MT," "7P6F," denotes the British Railways power classification.

"S" denotes Service (Departmental) locomotive still carrying B.R. number. This reference letter is introduced only for the reader's guidance and is not borne by the locomotive concerned.

The numbers of steam locomotives in service have been checked in L.M.R. to December 2, 1967; E.R. to December 30, 1967; N.E.R. to November 4, 1967; Sc.R. to November 25, 1967; S.R. to November 13, 1967; and W.R. to December 4, 1967.

Ex-G.W.R. STEAM LOCOMOTIVES

Unclass.   V. of R.   2-6-2T

Introduced 1902. Davies and Metcalfe design for Vale of Rheidol
1' 11½" gauge.
*Introduced 1923. G.W. development of Vale of Rheidol design.

Weight
25 tons

Gauge
1' 11½"

Boiler pressure
165 lb sq in NS

Cylinders
(O) 11" × 17"
(O) 11½" × 17" *

Driving wheel diameter
2' 6"

Tractive effort
9,615 lb
10,510 lb *

Valve gear
Walschaerts

7 *	Owain Glyndŵr	9	Prince of Wales
8 *	Llywelyn		

TOTAL: 3

LOCOMOTIVE SUPERINTENDENTS AND CHIEF MECHANICAL ENGINEERS
G.W.R.

Sir Daniel Gooch	...	1837–1864	William Dean	1877–1902
Joseph Armstrong	... {	1854–1864* / 1864–1877	G. J. Churchward ...	1902–1921
			Charles B. Collett ...	1922–1941
George Armstrong	...	1864–1896*	F. W. Hawksworth ...	1941–1949

*In charge of standard gauge locomotives at Stafford Road Works, Wolverhampton, with wide powers in design and construction.

Vale of Rheidol 2-6-2T No. 9 *Prince of Wales* at Aberystwyth

[K. R. Pirt

EX-L.M.S. STEAM LOCOMOTIVES

4MT   2-6-0

Introduced 1947. Ivatt L.M.S. taper boiler design with double chimney. Later engines introduced with single chimney with which earlier engines have been rebuilt.

Weight
Locomotive: 59 tons 2 cwt

Driving wheel diameter
5′ 3″

Boiler pressure
225 lb sq in

Tractive effort
24,170 lb

Cylinders
(O) 17½″ × 26″

Valve gear
Walschaerts (piston valves)

43002	43008	43019	43027	43047	43088	43106
43006	43010	43023	43033			

TOTAL: 11

5MT   4-6-0

Introduced 1934. Stanier L.M.S. taper boiler design.

Experimental locomotives:

Introduced 1947[1]. Stephenson link motion (outside), Timken roller bearings.

Introduced 1947[2]. Timken roller bearings.

Introduced 1950[3]. Skefko roller bearings.

Introduced 1950[4]. Timken roller bearings on driving coupled axle only.

Introduced 1950[5]. Skefko roller bearings on driving coupled axle only.

Weight
Locomotive: 72 tons 2 cwt
               75 tons 6 cwt ([1,2,3,4,5])

Driving wheel diameter
6′ 0″

Boiler pressure
225 lb sq in

Tractive effort
25,455 lb

Cylinders
(O) 18½″ × 28″

Valve gear
Walschaerts (piston valves) except where otherwise shown

Ivatt Class 4MT 2-6-
No. 43106
[A. D. McIntyr

Outside Stephenson
valve gear of Cla
5MT 4-6-0 No. 4476
[D. L. Percive

Class 5MT 4-6-0 No
44899 (with top-feed
on leading boile
section)
[H. L. Hollan

44663	44761²	44818	44874	44910	44988	45073
44664	44767¹	44829	44877	44915	44993	45076
44665	44773	44834	44878	44916	45001	45083
44672⁶	44777	44836	44884	44926	45005	45092
44674⁵	44780	44838	44887	44929	45013	45095
44683³	44781	44842	44888	44932	45017	45096
44690⁴	44800	44845	44889	44940	45025	45101
44708	44802	44846	44890	44942	45027	45104
44709	44803	44848	44891	44947	45034	45110
44711	44804	44851	44894	44949	45038	45114
44713	44806	44855	44895	44950	45041	45131
44715	44807	44858	44897	44962	45046	45133
44728	44809	44864	44899	44963	45054	45134
44734	44815	44868	44903	44965	45055	45149
44735	44816	44871	44906	44971	45065	45150
44758²						

45156 *Ayrshire Yeomanry*

45187	45221	45260	45294	45345	45390	45421
45190	45227	45262	45295	45350	45391	45424
45196	45231	45268	45296	45353	45392	45426
45200	45236	45269	45305	45375	45394	45435
45201	45246	45279	45310	45376	45395	45436
45202	45253	45282	45312	45377	45397	45444
45203	45254	45284	45316	45381	45407	45445
45206	45255	45285	45318	45382	45411	45447
45209	45258	45287	45330	45386	45420	45493
45212	45259	45290	45342	45388		

TOTAL: 175

8F   2-8-0

Introduced 1935. Stanier L.M.S. taper boiler design.

Weight
Locomotive: 72 tons 2 cwt

Boiler pressure
225 lb sq in

Cylinders
(O) 18½″ × 28″

Driving wheel diameter
4′ 8½″

Tractive effort
32,440 lb

Valve gear
Walschaerts (piston valves)

33

Class 5MT 4-6-0 No. 44906 (with top-feed on second boiler section) [G. W. Morrison

Class 5MT 4-6-0 No. 45156 *Ayrshire Yeomanry* (with combined dome and top-feed)
[D. P. Williams

Class 8F 2-8-0 No. 48060 [P. L. Simpson

48010	48170	48304	48365	48453	48559	48700
48012	48182	48305	48368	48465	48609	48702
48026	48190	48307	48369	48467	48612	48715
48033	48191	48308	48373	48468	48614	48720
48036	48192	48310	48374	48469	48617	48722
48045	48193	48317	48380	48471	48620	48723
48046	48197	48319	48384	48476	48626	48727
48056	48200	48321	48390	48491	48631	48729
48060	48201	48322	48392	48492	48632	48730
48062	48205	48323	48393	48493	48639	48740
48063	48206	48325	48400	48503	48646	48744
48077	48212	48327	48402	48504	48652	48745
48081	48224	48329	48410	48507	48665	48746
48090	48247	48334	48421	48510	48666	48749
48107	48252	48335	48423	48519	48674	48750
48111	48253	48336	48424	48529	48677	48752
48115	48257	48338	48433	48532	48678	48757
48117	48267	48340	48436	48533	48683	48758
48124	48272	48344	48437	48544	48684	48763
48132	48278	48345	48441	48546	48687	48764
48151	48282	48348	48442	48549	48692	48765
48153	48292	48351	48445	48551	48696	48773
48167	48293	48356	48448	48553	48697	48775
48168	48294	48362	48451			

TOTAL: 165

LOCOMOTIVE SUPERINTENDENTS AND CHIEF MECHANICAL ENGINEERS
L.M.S.

George Hughes	1923–1925	Sir William Stanier ... 1932–1944
Sir Henry Fowler ...	1925–1931	Charles E. Fairburn ... 1944–1945
E. H. J. Lemon		H. G. Ivatt 1945–1951
(Sir Ernest Lemon)	1931–1932	

CALEDONIAN

Robert Sinclair		
(First Loco. engineer)		1847–1856
Benjamin Connor	...	1856–1876
George Brittain	...	1876–1882
Dugald Drummond	...	1882–1890
Hugh Smellie	... ...	1890
J. Lambie	...	1890–1895
J. F. McIntosh	...	1895–1914
William Pickersgill	...	1914–1923

GLASGOW & SOUTH WESTERN

Patrick Stirling ...	...	1853–1866
James Stirling	...	1866–1878
Hugh Smellie	...	1878–1890
James Manson ...	...	1890–1912
Peter Drummond	...	1912–1918
R. H. Whitelegg	...	1918–1923

HIGHLAND

William Stroudley (First loco engineer) ...	1866–1869
David Jones	1869–1896
Peter Drummond ...	1896–1911
F. G. Smith	1912–1915
C. Cumming	1915–1923

NORTH STAFFORDSHIRE

L. Clare	1876–1882
L. Longbottom	1882–1902
J. H. Adams	1902–1915
J. A. Hookham	1915–1923

W. Angus was Loco. Supt. at Stoke prior to 1876. No earlier records can be traced.

LANCASHIRE & YORKSHIRE

Sir John Hawkshaw (Consultant), Hurst and Jenkins successively to 1868

W. Hurst	1868–1876
W. Barton Wright ...	1876–1886
John A. F. Aspinall ...	1886–1899
H. A. Hoy	1899–1904
George Hughes	1904–1921

The L. & Y. amalgamated with L.N.W.R. as from January 1st, 1922

LONDON & NORTH WESTERN

Francis Trevithick and J. E. McConnell, first loco. engineers, 1846, with Alexander Allan largely responsible for design at Crewe.

John Ramsbottom ...	1857–1871
Francis William Webb ...	1871–1903
George Whale	1903–1909
Charles John Bowen-Cooke ...	1909–1920
Capt. Hewitt Pearson Montague Beames ...	1920–1921
George Hughes	1922

FURNESS

R. Mason	1890–1897
W. F. Pettigrew	1897–1918
D. J. Rutherford	1918–1923

SOMERSET & DORSET JOINT

Until leased by Mid. and L. & S. W. (as from 1st November 1875) locomotives were bought from outside builders, principally George England of Hatcham Iron Works, S.E. After the above date, Derby and its various Loco. Supts. and C.M.Es. have acted for S. & D.J. aided by a resident Loco. Supt. stationed at Highbridge Works.

MIDLAND

Matthew Kirtley (First loco. engineer)	1844–1873
Samuel Waite Johnson	1873–1903
Richard Mountford Deeley	1903–1909
Henry Fowler	1909–1923

NORTH LONDON

(Worked by L. & N.W. by agreement dated December, 1908.)

William Adams	1853–1873
J. C. Park	1873–1893
Henry J. Pryce	1893–1908

MARYPORT & CARLISLE

Hugh Smellie	1870–1878
J. Campbell	1878–
William Coulthard ...	* –1904
J. B. Adamson	1904–1923

WIRRAL

Eric G. Barker	1892–1902
T. B. Hunter	1903–1923

LONDON, TILBURY & SOUTHEND

Thomas Whitelegg ...	1880–1910
Robert Harben Whitelegg	1910–1912

(L.T. & S.R. absorbed by M.R. and control of locos transferred to Derby as from August, 1912.)

---

*Date of actual entry into office not known.

Ex-L.N.E.R. STEAM LOCOMOTIVES

5P6F   **K I**   **2-6-0**

Introduced 1949. Peppercorn development of Thompson K1/1 (rebuilt from Gresley K4) with increased length.

Weight
Locomotive: 66 tons 17 cwt
Tender: 44 tons 4 cwt

Boiler pressure
225 lb sq in

Cylinders
(O) 20″ × 26″

Driving wheel diameter
5′ 2″

Tractive effort
32,080 lb

Valve gear
Walschaerts (piston valves)

62005

TOTAL: I

ROUTE AVAILABILITY OF LOCOMOTIVES

R.A. No.	Ex-L.N.E.R.	Ex-L.M.S.	B.R.
4		4MT (2-6-0).	
6	K I.	8F.	
7		5MT (4-6-0).	4MT (4-6-0), 5MT (4-6-0).
8			7MT (4-6-2).
9			9F (2-10-0).

[D. L. Percival]

Class K1 2-6-0 No. 62005 at West Hartlepool with empty stock for an SLS special

38

LOCOMOTIVE SUPERINTENDENTS AND CHIEF MECHANICAL ENGINEERS

L.N.E.R.

Sir Nigel Gresley	...	1923–1941
A. H. Peppercorn	...	1946–1949
E. Thompson	... ...	1941–1946

GREAT NORTHERN

A. Sturrock	... ...	1850–1866
P. Stirling	... ...	1866–1895
H. A. Ivatt	... ...	1896–1911
H. N. Gresley	... ...	1911–1922

NORTH EASTERN

E. Fletcher	... ...	1854–1883
A. McDonnell*	... ...	1883–1884
T. W. Worsdell	... ...	1885–1890
W. Worsdell	... ...	1890–1910
Sir Vincent Raven	...	1910–1922

GREAT EASTERN

R. Sinclair	... ...	1862–1866
S. W. Johnson	... ...	1866–1873
W. Adams	... ...	1873–1878
M. Bromley	... ...	1878–1881
T. W. Worsdell	... ...	1881–1885
J. Holden	... ...	1885–1907
S. D. Holden	... ...	1908–1912
A. J. Hill	... ...	1912–1922

LANCASHIRE, DERBYSHIRE AND EAST COAST

R. A. Thom	...	1902–1907

MANCHESTER, SHEFFIELD AND LINCOLNSHIRE

Richard Peacock	...	–1854
W. G. Craig	... ...	1854–1859

Charles Sacré	... ...	1859–1886
T. Parker	... ...	1886–1893
H. Pollitt	... ...	1893–1897

GREAT CENTRAL

H. Pollitt	... ...	1897–1900
J. G. Robinson	... ...	1900–1922

HULL AND BARNSLEY

M. Stirling	... ...	1885–1922

MIDLAND AND GREAT NORTHERN JOINT

W. Marriott	... ...	1884–1924

NORTH BRITISH

T. Wheatley†	... ...	1867–1874
D. Drummond	... ...	1875–1882
M. Holmes	... ...	1882–1903
W. P. Reid	... ...	1903–1919
W. Chalmers	... ...	1919–1922

GREAT NORTH OF SCOTLAND

D. K. Clark	... ...	1853–1855
J. F. Ruthven	... ...	1855–1857
W. Cowan	... ...	1857–1883
J. Manson	... ...	1883–1890
J. Johnson	... ...	1890–1894
W. Pickersgill	... ...	1894–1914
T. E. Heywood	... ...	1914–1922

* Between McDonnell and T. W. Worsdell there was an interval during which the office was covered by a Locomotive Committee.

† Previous to whom the records are indeterminate.

Standard Class 7P6F No. 70051 *Firth of Forth*   [*F. R. Sherlock*

Standard Class 5MT 4-6-0 No. 73000   [*N. E. Preedy*

Standard Class 5MT 4-6-0 No. 73126 (with Caprotti valve gear)   [*G. H. Wheeler*

B.R. STANDARD STEAM LOCOMOTIVES

7P6F   4-6-2

Introduced 1951. Designed at Derby.

Weight
Locomotive: 94 tons 4 cwt

Driving wheel diameter
6' 2"

Boiler pressure
250 lb sq in

Tractive effort
32,150 lb

Cylinders
(O) 20" × 28"

Valve gear
Walschaerts (piston valves)

70004	William Shakespeare	70023	Venus
70011	Hotspur	70024	Vulcan
70012	John of Gaunt	70025	Western Star
70013	Oliver Cromwell	70035	Rudyard Kipling
70014	Iron Duke	70045	Lord Rowallan
70021	Morning Star	70049	Solway Firth
70022	Tornado	70051	Firth of Forth

TOTAL: 14

5MT   4-6-0

Introduced 1951. Designed at Doncaster.
*Introduced 1956. Fitted with Caprotti valve gear.

Weight
Locomotive: 76 tons 4 cwt

Driving wheel diameter
6' 2"

Boiler pressure
225 lb sq in

Tractive effort
26,120 lb

Cylinders
(O) 19" × 28"

Valve gear
Walschaerts (piston valves)

73000	73035	73067	73126*	73132*	73135*	73142*
73010	73040	73069	73128*	73133*	73136*	73143*
73033	73050	73125*	73131*	73134*	73138*	73157
73034	73053					

TOTAL: 23

Standard Class 4MT 4-6-0 No. 75030   [J. C. Haydon

Standard Class 9F 2-10-0 No. 92091   [M. York

Standard Class 9F 2-10-0 No. 92249 (with double chimney)   [A. W. Martin

4MT

4-6-0

Introduced 1951. Designed at Brighton.
*Introduced 1957. Fitted with double chimney.

Weight
Locomotive: 69 tons

Driving wheel diameter
5′ 8″

Boiler pressure
225 lb sq in

Tractive effort
25,100 lb

Cylinders
(O) 18″ × 28″

Valve gear
Walschaerts (piston valves)

75009	75020*	75027	75033	75037	75043	75058
75015	75021	75030	75034	75041	75048	75062
75019	75026*	75032				

TOTAL: 17

9F

2-10-0

Introduced 1954. Designed at Brighton.
*Introduced 1957. Fitted with double chimney.

Weight
Locomotive: 86 tons 14 cwt

Driving wheel diameter
5′ 0″

Boiler pressure
250 lb sq in

Tractive effort
39,670 lb

Cylinders
(O) 20″ × 28″

Valve gear
Walschaerts (piston valves)

92004	92055	92091	92118	92160	92204*	92223*
92009	92069	92094	92125	92165*	92212*	92233*
92017	92077	92110	92153	92167*	92218*	92249*
92054	92088	92117				

TOTAL: 24

BRITISH RAILWAYS STANDARD TENDERS

N.B.—*These pairings are not permanent and are liable to alteration with changed operating conditions.*

Type	Capacity Water galls	Coal tons	Weight in full W.O. tons	cwt	Locomotives to which originally allocated
BRI ...	4,250	7	49	3	70000–24/30–44 72000–9 73000–49
BRIA ...	5,000	7	52	10	70025–9
BRIB ...	4,725	7	50	5	92020–9/60–6/97–99 73080–9 73100–9/20–34/45–71 75065–79 76053–69
BRIC ...	4,725	9	53	5	92015–9/45–59/77–86 92100–39/50–64 73065–79/90–9 73135–44
BRID ...	4,725	9	54	10	70045–54
BRIF ...	5,625	7	55	5	92010–4/30–44/67–76 92087–96 92140–9/68–92202 73110–9
BRIG ...	5,000	7	52	10	92000–9 73050–2 92203–50
BRIH ...	4,250	7	49	3	73053–64
BRIK ...	4,325	9	52	7	92165–7
BR2 ...	3,500	6	42	3	75000–49 76000–44
BR2A ...	3,500	6	42	3	75050–64 76045–52/70–76114 77000–19
BR3 ...	3,000	4	36	17	78000–64

LOCOMOTIVES PRESERVED

Date built	Previous owner	Type	Locomotive	Place of preservation
1822	Hetton Colliery	0-4-0		York Railway Museum
1825	Stockton & Darlington	0-4-0	Locomotion	Darlington Bank Top Station
1829	Shutt End Railway	0-4-0	Agenoria	York Railway Museum
1837	G.W.R.	2-2-2	North Star	Swindon Museum
	Grand Junction	2-2-2	No. 49 Columbine	York Railway Museum
1845	Stockton & Darlington	0-6-0	No. 25 Derwent	Darlington Bank Top Station
1846	Furness	0-4-0	No. 3 Coppernob	Clapham Museum
1847	L.N.W.R.	2-2-2	No. 3020 Cornwall	Clapham Museum
1857	Wantage Tramway	0-4-0WT	No. 5 Shannon	Wantage
1865	L.N.W.R.	18" gauge 0-4-0T	Pet	Clapham Museum
1865	L.N.W.R.	0-4-0ST	No. 1439	Crewe Works
1866	M.R.	2-4-0 Class 1	No. 158A	Hellifield
1866	Metropolitan	4-4-0T Class A	No. 23	Clapham Museum
1868	South Devon	Broad gauge 0-4-0T	Tiny	Newton Abbot Station
1869	N.E.R.	2-2-4T	No. 66 Aerolite	York Railway Museum
1870	G.N.R.	4-2-2	No. 1	York Railway Museum
1872	Metropolitan	0-4-0 Tram Locomotive	No. 807	Clapham Museum
1874	N.E.R.	0-6-0	No. 1275	York Railway Museum
1875	N.E.R.	2-4-0 901 Class	No. 910	York Railway Museum
1880	L.B.S.C.R.	0-6-0T Class A	No. 82 Boxhill	Clapham Museum
1882	L.B.S.C.R.	0-4-2 Class B1	No. 214 Gladstone	York Railway Museum
1885	Mersey Railway	0-6-4T	No. 5 Cecil Raikes	City of Liverpool Museum
1885	N.E.R.	2-4-0 1463 Class	No. 1463	York Railway Museum
1886	C.R.	4-2-2	No. 123	Glasgow Transport Museum
1887	L.Y.R.	18" gauge 0-4-0T	Wren	Clapham Museum
1889	L.Y.R.	2-4-2T Class K2	No. 1008	Stratford Works

(continued)

Date built	Previous owner	Type	Locomotive	Place of preservation
1892	L.N.W.R.	2-4-0 'President' Class	No. 790 Hardwicke	Clapham Museum
1893	N.E.R.	4-4-0 Class MI	No. 1621	York Railway Museum
1893	L.S.W.R.	4-4-0 Class T3	No. 563	Clapham Museum
1893	Shropshire and Montgomeryshire	0-4-0WT	Gazelle	Longmoor
1894	H.R.	4-6-0	No. 103	Glasgow Transport Museum
1895	G.E.R.	2-4-0 Class T26	No. 490	Clapham Museum
1897	G.W.R.	0-6-0 2301 Class	No. 2516	Swindon Museum
1898	G.N.R.	4-4-2	No. 990 Henry Oakley	York Railway Museum
1899	M.R.	4-2-2 115 Class	No. 118	Hellifield
1899	L.S.W.R.	4-4-0 Class T9	No. 120	Stratford Works
1901	S.E.C.R.	4-4-0 Class D	No. 737	Clapham Museum
1902	M.R.	4-4-0 Class 4	No. 1000	Clapham Museum
1902	G.N.R.	4-4-2 Class CI	No. 251	York Railway Museum
1903	G.W.R.	2-8-0 28XX Class	No. 2818	Bristol City Museum
1904	G.E.R.	0-6-0T Class S56	No. 87	Clapham Museum
1905	G.E.R.	0-6-0 Class G58	No. 1217	Hellifield
1907	G.W.R.	4-6-0 'Star' Class	No. 4003 Lode Star	Swindon Museum
1909	L.T.S.R.	4-4-2T 79 Class	No. 80 Thundersley	Hellifield
1913	N.B.R.	4-4-0 'Glen' Class	No. 256 Glen Douglas	Glasgow Transport Museum
1920	G.N.S.R.	4-4-0 Class F	No. 49 Gordon Highlander	Glasgow Transport Museum
1920	G.C.R.	4-4-0 Class 11F	No. 506 Butler-Henderson	Clapham Museum
1923	G.W.R.	4-6-0 'Castle' Class	No. 4073 Caerphilly Castle	Science Museum, London
1936	L.N.E.R.	2-6-2 Class V2	No. 4771 Green Arrow	Hellifield
1937	L.M.S.	4-6-2 Class 7P	No. 46235 City of Birmingham	Birmingham Museum of Science and Industry
1938	L.N.E.R.	4-6-2 Class A4	No. 4468 Mallard	Clapham Museum
1947	G.W.R.	0-6-0PT 94XX Class	No. 9400	Swindon Museum

Right: 6000 Class 4-6-0 No. 6000 *King George V*
[D. L. Percival

Centre: Class T9 4-4-0 No. 120
[D. L. Percival

Bottom: Standard Class 7P6F 4-6-2 No. 70000 *Britannia*
[K. R. Pirt

47

LOCOMOTIVES SCHEDULED FOR PRESERVATION

Date built	Previous owner	Type	Locomotive
1874	L.S.W.R.	2-4-0WT 0298 Class	No. 298 (*30587)
1891	N.E.R.	0-6-0 Class C	No. 1576 (*65099)
1897	L.S.W.R.	0-4-4T Class M7	No. 245 (*30245)
1897	T.V.R.	0-6-2T	No. 28
1911	G.C.R.	2-8-0 Class O4	No. 102 (*63601)
1917	G.S.W.R.	0-6-0T	No. 9
1919	N.E.R.	0-8-0 Class T3	No. 901 (*63460)
1921	L.N.W.R.	0-8-0 Class G2	No. 485 (*49395)
1922	N.S.R.	0-6-2T	No. 2
1924	L.M.S.	0-6-0 Class 4F	No. 4027 (*44027)
1926	S.R.	4-6-0 'Lord Nelson' Class	No. E850 Lord Nelson (*30850)
1926	L.M.S.	2-6-0 Class 5	No. 13000 (*42700)
1927	G.W.R.	4-6-0 'King' Class	*No. 6000 King George V
1930	S.R.	4-4-0 'Schools' Class	No. 925 Cheltenham (*30925)
1934	L.M.S.	4-6-0 Class 5	No. 5000 (*45000)
1935	L.M.S.	2-6-4T Class 4 (3-cyl.)	No. 2500 (*42500)
1942	S.R.	0-6-0 Class Q1	No. C1 (*33001)
1945	S.R.	4-6-2 'West Country' Class	No. 21C151 Winston Churchill (*34051)
1951	B.R.	4-6-2 Class 7	*No. 70000 Britannia
1956	B.R.	4-6-0 Class 5 (with Caprotti valve gear)	

*B.R.number. Withdrawn from service but not yet restored for preservation.

B.R. DIESEL LOCOMOTIVES

BRITISH RAILWAYS diesel locomotives are listed in this publication in numerical order and classified by make. In 1957 the then British Transport Commission announced a new numbering system for all diesel locomotives, involving the use of the prefix "D" for all such locomotives, followed by a number which would not only identify the locomotive, but would also indicate its power range; at the same time, the power of main-line locomotives was to be indicated by Type numbers in the following ranges:—

Type of Locomotive	Horsepower
1	800–1,000
2	1,000–1,365
3	1,500–1,750
4	2,000–2,750
5	3,000+

Subsequently, new batches of locomotives have been delivered and numbered outside the original groups for the type so that it is not always possible to ascertain the power of a locomotive solely by its number. Locomotives built before nationalisation, or after nationalisation to company designs, are numbered in a separate series commencing at 10000 without a prefix "D". Early British Railways diesel shunters were numbered in this series but have since been renumbered into the "D" series.

The heading to each class shows the type designation, the principal manufacturer and the wheel arrangement.

Diesel (and electric) locomotive wheel arrangements are described by a development of the Continental notation. This calculates by axles and not by wheels, and uses letters instead of numerals to denote driving axles ("A" = 1, "B" = 2, "C" = 3, etc.) and numerals only for non-powered axles. An indication of the grouping of axles is given, but powered and non-powered axles may be found in the same group. Thus, diesel-electric locomotive No. D5500 is described as an A1A-A1A, indicating that it is mounted on two six-wheel bogies, each of which has a non-powered axle in the centre and a motored axle at either end. Groups of axles are separated by a hyphen if they are quite independent of each other, but by a "plus" sign in cases where powered bogies are linked by an articulated joint to take certain stresses. If all axles on a bogie or frame unit are individually powered, a suffix letter "o" is added to the descriptive letter.

The sub-headings give brief technical details of each type. Reference marks are shown in the details and against the locomotives concerned (if known) where equipment varies from the main batch.

COUPLING OF DIESEL LOCOMOTIVES

*Although several diesel locomotives may be coupled together
and driven by one man in the leading cab, for various reasons
it is not possible for all types of diesel units to work together.
In order to distinguish locomotives that can run together, all have
painted above each buffer a colour code symbol. This is repeated
as a miniature symbol on the plug socket covers. Only units
bearing the same symbol may run in multiple and be controlled
from the leading cab.*

Type of Locomotive	*Coupling symbol*
All diesel-electric locomotives with electro-pneumatic control	Blue star ★
All diesel-electric locomotives with electro-magnetic control.	Red circle ●
Diesel-hydraulic locomotives Nos. D600-4, D6300-5.	Orange square □
Diesel-hydraulic locomotives Nos. D803-70, D6306-57 (Nos. D800-2 cannot work in multiple).	White diamond ◇
Diesel-hydraulic locomotives Nos. D7000-7100.	Yellow triangle △
Diesel-electric locomotives Nos. D8500-8587.	Red diamond ◆

DIESEL LOCOMOTIVES

The lists of numbers include all locomotives on order at the time of going to press.

Type 4	**British Railways**	**ICo-Col**
	"Peak"	★

Introduced
1959

Engine
*Sulzer 12-cyl 12LDA28-A twin-bank pressure charged of 2,300 b.h.p. at 750 r.p.m.
Sulzer 12LDA28-B, with inter-cooling of 2,500 b.h.p. at 750 r.p.m.

Weight
138 tons 2 cwt

Maximum tractive effort
70,000 lb

Total b.h.p.
2,300*
2,500

Transmission
Electric. Six Crompton Parkinson 305 h.p. axle-hung nose-suspended traction motors
†Six Brush traction motors

Driving wheel diameter
3' 9"

D1* Scafell Pike	D6* Whernside	
D2* Helvellyn	D7* Ingleborough	
D3* Skiddaw	D8* Penyghent	
D4* Great Gable	D9* Snowdon	
D5* Cross Fell	D10* Tryfan	

D11	D17	D23	D29	D34	D39	D44
D12	D18	D24	D30	D35	D40	D45
D13	D19	D25	D31	D36	D41	D46
D14	D20	D26	D32	D37	D42	D47
D15	D21	D27	D33	D38	D43	D48
D16	D22	D28				

D49	The Manchester Regiment	D60	Lytham St. Annes
D50	King's Shropshire Light Infantry	D61	Royal Army Ordnance Corps
D51		D62	5th Royal Inniskilling Dragoon Guards
D52	The Lancashire Fusilier		
D53	Royal Tank Regiment	D63	Royal Inniskilling Fusilier
D54	The Royal Pioneer Corps	D64	Coldstream Guardsman
D55	Royal Signals	D65	Grenadier Guardsman
D56	The Bedfordshire and Hertfordshire Regiment (T.A.)	D66	
		D67	Royal Artilleryman
		D68	Royal Fusilier
D57		D69	
D58	The King's Own Royal Border Regiment	D70	Royal Marines
		D71	
D59	The Royal Warwickshire Fusilier	D72	
		D73	

51

British Railways Type 4 2,300 b.h.p. diesel-electric 1Co-Col No. D7 *Ingleborough*
[*D. L. Percival*

Nameplate of British Railways Type 4 2,500 b.h.p. diesel-electric 1Co-Col No. D77
Royal Irish Fusilier
[*D. L. Percival*

British Railways Type 4 2,500 b.h.p. diesel-electric 1Co-Col No. D162 (in blue livery)
[*D. L. Percival*

D74	D75	D76

D77 *Royal Irish Fusilier*

D78	D79	D80	D81	D82	D83

D84 *Royal Corps of Transport*

D85	D86	D87	D88

D89 *Honourable Artillery Company*

D90	D92	D94	D95	D96	D97
D91	D93				

D98 *Royal Engineer*   D99 *3rd Carabinier*

D100 *Sherwood Forester*

D101	D110	D119	D128	D137	D146†	D155†
D102	D111	D120	D129	D138†	D147†	D156†
D103	D112	D121	D130	D139†	D148†	D157†
D104	D113	D122	D131	D140†	D149†	D158†
D105	D114	D123	D132	D141†	D150†	D159†
D106	D115	D124	D133	D142†	D151†	D160†
D107	D116	D125	D134	D143†	D152†	D161†
D108	D117	D126	D135	D144†	D153†	D162†
D109	D118	D127	D136	D145†	D154†	

D163† *Leicestershire and Derbyshire Yeomanry*

D164†	D169†	D174†	D178†	D182†	D186†	D190†
D165†	D170†	D175†	D179†	D183†	D187†	D191†
D166†	D171†	D176†	D180†	D184†	D188†	D192†
D167†	D172†	D177†	D181†	D185†	D189†	D193†
D168†	D173†					

TOTAL: 193

Type 4   English Electric   1Co-Co1

Introduced
1958

Total b.h.p.
2,000   ★

Engine
English Electric 16-cyl 16SVT Mk. II
of 2,000 b.h.p. at 850 r.p.m.

Transmission
Electric. Six English Electric nose
suspended traction motors

Weight
133 tons

Driving wheel diameter
3′ 9″

Maximum tractive effort
52,000 lb

D200	D202	D204	D206	D207	D208	D209
D201	D203	D205				

D210	*Empress of Britain*		D217	*Carinthia*
D211	*Mauretania*		D218	*Carmania*
D212	*Aureol*		D219	*Caronia*
D213	*Andania*		D220	*Franconia*
D214	*Antonia*		D221	*Ivernia*
D215	*Aquitania*		D222	*Laconia*
D216	*Campania*		D223	*Lancastria*

English Electric Type 4 2,000 b.h.p. diesel-electric 1Co-Co1 No. D270 (in blue livery)
[*D. L. Percival*

English Electric Type 4 2,000 b.h.p. diesel-electric 1Co-Co1 No. D395
[*Eric Treacy*

English Electric Type 4 2,700 b.h.p. diesel-electric Co-Co No. D400 (in blue livery)
[*English Electric*

D224	Lucania			D230	Scythia
D225	Lusitania			D231	Sylvania
D226				D232	Empress of Canada
D227	Parthia			D233	Empress of England
D228	Samaria			D234	Accra
D229	Saxonia			D235	Apapa

D236	D260	D284	D308	D331	D354	D377
D237	D261	D285	D309	D332	D355	D378
D238	D262	D286	D310	D333	D356	D379
D239	D263	D287	D311	D334	D357	D380
D240	D264	D288	D312	D335	D358	D381
D241	D265	D289	D313	D336	D359	D382
D242	D266	D290	D314	D337	D360	D383
D243	D267	D291	D315	D338	D361	D384
D244	D268	D292	D316	D339	D362	D385
D245	D269	D293	D317	D340	D363	D386
D246	D270	D294	D318	D341	D364	D387
D247	D271	D295	D319	D342	D365	D388
D248	D272	D296	D320	D343	D366	D389
D249	D273	D297	D321	D344	D367	D390
D250	D274	D298		D345	D368	D391
D251	D275	D299	D323	D346	D369	D392
D252	D276	D300	D324	D347	D370	D393
D253	D277	D301	D325	D348	D371	D394
D254	D278	D302	D326	D349	D372	D395
D255	D279	D303	D327	D350	D373	D396
D256	D280	D304	D328	D351	D374	D397
D257	D281	D305	D329	D352	D375	D398
D258	D282	D306	D330	D353	D376	D399
D259	D283	D307				**TOTAL: 199**

Type 4   English Electric   Co-Co

Introduced
1967

Engine
English Electric 16-cyl 16CSVT, after-cooled, of 2,700 b.h.p.

Weight

Maximum tractive effort
48,500 lb

Total b.h.p.
2,700

Transmission
Electric. Six English Electric axle-hung, nose-suspended traction motors

Driving wheel diameter
3′ 7″

On hire to British Rail

D400	D408	D415	D422	D429	D436	D443
D401	D409	D416	D423	D430	D437	D444
D402	D410	D417	D424	D431	D438	D445
D403	D411	D418	D425	D432	D439	D446
D404	D412	D419	D426	D433	D440	D447
D405	D413	D420	D427	D434	D441	D448
D406	D414	D421	D428	D435	D442	D449
D407						**TOTAL: 50**

North British Type 4 2,000 b.h.p. diesel-hydraulic A1A-A1A No. D600 *Active* (in blue livery)
[*D. L. Percival*]

British Railways Type 4 2,200 b.h.p. diesel-hydraulic B-B No. D823 *Hermes*
[*A. D. McIntyre*]

Nameplate of British Railways Type 4 2,200 b.h.p. diesel-hydraulic B-B No. D825 *Intrepid*
[*D. L. Percival*]

56

Type 4   North British   A1A-A1A
"Warship"

Introduced
1958

Engines
Two N.B.L./M.A.N. 12-cyl L12V 18/21S of 1,000 b.h.p.

Weight
117 tons 8 cwt

Maximum tractive effort
50,000 lb

Total b.h.p.
2,000

Transmission
Hydraulic. Two Hardy Spicer cardan shafts to Voith-North British type L306r hydraulic transmissions, each containing three torque converters

Driving wheel diameter
3' 7"

D600	Active	D603	Conquest
D601	Ark Royal	D604	Cossack
D602	Bulldog		

TOTAL: 5

Type 4   British Railways   B-B
"Warship"   ◊

Introduced
1958

Engines
Two Bristol Siddeley-Maybach MD 650 V-type of 1,152 b.h.p. at 1,530 r.p.m. (*1,056 b.h.p. at 1,400 r.p.m.) † Two Paxman 12-cyl high-speed 12 YJXL of 1,200 b.h.p. at 1,500 r.p.m.

Weight
78 tons

Maximum tractive effort
52,400 lb

Total b.h.p.
2,000*
2,200
2,400†

Transmission
Hydraulic. Two Mekydro type K104 hydraulic transmissions containing permanently filled single torque converter and four-speed automatic gearbox

Driving wheel diameter
3' 3½"

* These locomotives may not be coupled in multiple

D800*	Sir Brian Robertson	D816	Eclipse
D801*	Vanguard	D817	Foxhound
D802*	Formidable	D818	Glory
D803	Albion	D819	Goliath
D804	Avenger	D820	Grenville
D805	Benbow	D821	Greyhound
D806	Cambrian	D822	Hercules
D807	Caradoc	D823	Hermes
D808	Centaur	D824	Highflyer
D809	Champion	D825	Intrepid
D810	Cockade	D826	Jupiter
D811	Daring	D827	Kelly
D812	Royal Naval Reserve 1859-1959	D828	Magnificent
		D829	Magpie
D813	Diadem	D830†	Majestic
D814	Dragon	D831	Monarch
D815	Druid	D832	Onslaught

Class continued with D866

Type 4　　North British　　B-B

"Warship"

◇

Introduced
1960

Engines
Two N.B.L./M.A.N. 12-cyl L12V18/21BS of 1,100 b.h.p.

Weight
79 tons 10 cwt

Maximum tractive effort
53,400 lb

Total b.h.p.
2,200

Transmission
Hydraulic. Voith

Driving wheel diameter
3' 3½"

D833	Panther	D850	Swift
D834	Pathfinder	D851	Temeraire
D835	Pegasus	D852	Tenacious
D836	Powerful	D853	Thruster
D837	Ramillies	D854	Tiger
D838	Rapid	D855	Triumph
D839	Relentless	D856	Trojan
D840	Resistance	D857	Undaunted
D841	Roebuck	D858	Valorous
D842	Royal Oak	D859	Vanquisher
D843	Sharpshooter	D860	Victorious
D844	Spartan	D861	Vigilant
D845	Sprightly	D862	Viking
D846	Steadfast	D863	Warrior
D847	Strongbow	D864	Zambesi
D848	Sultan	D865	Zealous
D849	Superb		

TOTAL: 33

Type 4　　British Railways　　B-B

"Warship"

Class continued from D832

◇

D866	Zebra	D869	Zest
D867	Zenith	D870	Zulu
D868	Zephyr		

TOTAL: 38

Type 4   British Railways   C-C
"Western"

Introduced
1961

Total b.h.p.
2,700

Engines
Two Maybach MD655 V-type of 1,350 h.p. at 1,500 r.p.m.

Transmission
Hydraulic. Two Voith-North British L630rV hydraulic transmissions, each containing three torque converters

Weight
108 tons

Driving wheel diameter
3' 7"

Maximum tractive effort
72,600 lb

D1000	Western Enterprise	D1037	Western Empress
D1001	Western Pathfinder	D1038	Western Sovereign
D1002	Western Explorer	D1039	Western King
D1003	Western Pioneer	D1040	Western Queen
D1004	Western Crusader	D1041	Western Prince
D1005	Western Venturer	D1042	Western Princess
D1006	Western Stalwart	D1043	Western Duke
D1007	Western Talisman	D1044	Western Duchess
D1008	Western Harrier	D1045	Western Viscount
D1009	Western Invader	D1046	Western Marquis
D1010	Western Campaigner	D1047	Western Lord
D1011	Western Thunderer	D1048	Western Lady
D1012	Western Firebrand	D1049	Western Monarch
D1013	Western Ranger	D1050	Western Ruler
D1014	Western Leviathan	D1051	Western Ambassador
D1015	Western Champion	D1052	Western Viceroy
D1016	Western Gladiator	D1053	Western Patriarch
D1017	Western Warrior	D1054	Western Governor
D1018	Western Buccaneer	D1055	Western Advocate
D1019	Western Challenger	D1056	Western Sultan
D1020	Western Hero	D1057	Western Chieftain
D1021	Western Cavalier	D1058	Western Nobleman
D1022	Western Sentinel	D1059	Western Empire
D1023	Western Fusilier	D1060	Western Dominion
D1024	Western Huntsman	D1061	Western Envoy
D1025	Western Guardsman	D1062	Western Courier
D1026	Western Centurion	D1063	Western Monitor
D1027	Western Lancer	D1064	Western Regent
D1028	Western Hussar	D1065	Western Consort
D1029	Western Legionnaire	D1066	Western Prefect
D1030	Western Musketeer	D1067	Western Druid
D1031	Western Rifleman	D1068	Western Reliance
D1032	Western Marksman	D1069	Western Vanguard
D1033	Western Trooper	D1070	Western Gauntlet
D1034	Western Dragoon	D1071	Western Renown
D1035	Western Yeoman	D1072	Western Glory
D1036	Western Emperor	D1073	Western Bulwark

TOTAL: 74

North British Type 4 2,200 b.h.p. diesel-hydraulic B-B No. D851 *Temeraire*   [*C. Symes*

British Railways Type 4 2,700 b.h.p. diesel-hydraulic C-C No. D1000 *Western Enterprise* (in blue livery)   [*D. L. Percival*

British Railways Type 4 2,700 b.h.p. diesel-hydraulic C-C No. D1028 *Western Hussar*   [*N. E. Preedy*

Type 4　　　　Brush　　　　Co-Co

Introduced
1962

Engine
Sulzer 12-cyl 12LDA28-C twin-bank,
pressure-charged, of 2,750 b.h.p. at
800 r.p.m.
*Sulzer 12-cyl 12LVA24 of 2,650 b.h.p.
at 1,050 r.p.m.

Weight
114 tons

Maximum tractive effort
55,000 lb

Total b.h.p.
2,750
*2,650

Transmission
Electric. Six axle-hung, nose-
suspended Brush traction motors

Driving wheel diameter
3′ 9″

† Fitted with train air brake equipment

D1100†	D1513	D1538	D1563	D1588	D1612	D1636†
D1101†	D1514	D1539	D1564	D1589	D1613	D1637†
D1102†	D1515	D1540	D1565	D1590	D1614	D1638†
D1103†	D1516	D1541	D1566	D1591	D1615	D1639†
D1104†	D1517	D1542	D1567	D1592	D1616	D1640†
D1105†	D1518	D1543	D1568	D1593	D1617	D1641†
D1106†	D1519	D1544	D1569	D1594	D1618	D1642†
D1107†	D1520	D1545	D1570	D1595	D1619	D1643†
D1108†	D1521	D1546	D1571	D1596	D1620	D1644†
D1109†	D1522	D1547	D1572	D1597	D1621	D1645†
D1110†	D1523	D1548	D1573	D1598	D1622	D1646†
D1111†	D1524	D1549	D1574	D1599	D1623	D1647†
D1500	D1525	D1550	D1575	D1600	D1624	D1648†
D1501	D1526	D1551	D1576	D1601	D1625	D1649†
D1502	D1527	D1552	D1577	D1602	D1626	D1650†
D1503	D1528	D1553	D1578	D1603	D1627	D1651†
D1504	D1529	D1554	D1579	D1604	D1628	D1652†
D1505	D1530	D1555	D1580	D1605	D1629	D1653†
D1506	D1531	D1556	D1581	D1606	D1630	D1654†
D1507	D1532	D1557	D1582	D1607	D1631†	D1655†
D1508	D1533	D1558	D1583	D1608	D1632†	D1656†
D1509	D1534	D1559	D1584	D1609	D1633†	D1657†
D1510	D1535	D1560	D1585	D1610	D1634†	D1658†
D1511	D1536	D1561	D1586	D1611	D1635†	D1659†
D1512	D1537	D1562	D1587			

D1660†	City of Truro		D1668†	Orion
D1661†	North Star		D1669†	Python
D1662†	Isambard Kingdom Brunel		D1670†	
			D1672†	Colossus
D1663†	Sir Daniel Gooch		D1673†	Cyclops
D1664†	George Jackson Churchward		D1674†	Samson
			D1675†	Amazon
D1665†	Titan		D1676†	Vulcan
D1666†	Odin		D1677†	Thor
D1667†	Atlas			

Top: Brush Type
2,750 b.h.p. diesel
electric   1Co-Co
Nos. D1662 *Isambard
Kingdom Brunel* and
D1667 *Atlas*
[*D. L. Percival*

Centre: Brush Type
2,750 b.h.p. diesel
electric 1Co-Co1 No.
D1846
[*D. L. Percival*

Left: Drewry 204
b.h.p.   diesel-mech
anical   0-6-0   No.
D2205
[*A. D. McIntyre*

62

D1678†	D1724	D1771†	D1817†	D1863†	D1909†	D1955†
D1679†	D1725	D1772†	D1818†	D1864†	D1910†	D1956†
D1680†	D1726	D1773†	D1819†	D1865†	D1911†	D1957†
D1681†	D1727	D1774†	D1820†	D1866†	D1912†	D1958†
D1682	D1728	D1775†	D1821†	D1867†	D1913†	D1959†
D1683	D1729	D1776†	D1822†	D1868†	D1914†	D1960†
D1684	D1730	D1777†	D1823†	D1869†	D1915†	D1961†
D1685	D1731	D1778†	D1824†	D1870†	D1916†	D1962†
D1686	D1732	D1779†	D1825†	D1871†	D1917†	D1963†
D1687	D1733	D1780†	D1826†	D1872†	D1918†	D1964†
D1688	D1735	D1781†	D1827†	D1873†	D1919†	D1965†
D1689	D1736	D1782†	D1828†	D1874†	D1920†	D1966†
D1690	D1737	D1783†	D1829†	D1875†	D1921†	D1967†
D1691	D1738	D1784†	D1830†	D1876†	D1922†	D1968†
D1692	D1739	D1785†	D1831†	D1877†	D1923†	D1969†
D1693	D1740	D1786†	D1832†	D1878†	D1924†	D1970†
D1694	D1741	D1787†	D1833†	D1879†	D1925†	D1971†
D1695	D1742	D1788†	D1834†	D1880†	D1926†	D1972†
D1696	D1743	D1789†	D1835†	D1881†	D1927†	D1973†
D1697	D1744	D1790†	D1836†	D1882†	D1928†	D1974†
D1698	D1745	D1791†	D1837†	D1883†	D1929†	D1975†
D1699	D1746	D1792†	D1838†	D1884†	D1930†	D1976†
D1700	D1747	D1793†	D1839†	D1885†	D1931†	D1977†
D1701	D1748	D1794†	D1840†	D1886†	D1932†	D1978†
D1702*	D1749	D1795†	D1841†	D1887†	D1933†	D1979†
D1703*	D1750	D1796†	D1842†	D1888†	D1934†	D1980†
D1704*	D1751	D1797†	D1843†	D1889†	D1935†	D1981†
D1705*	D1752	D1798†	D1844†	D1890†	D1936†	D1982†
D1706*	D1753	D1799†	D1845†	D1891†	D1937†	D1983†
D1707	D1754	D1800†	D1846†	D1892†	D1938†	D1984†
D1708	D1755	D1801†	D1847†	D1893†	D1939†	D1985†
D1709	D1756	D1802†	D1848†	D1894†	D1940†	D1986†
D1710	D1757	D1803†	D1849†	D1895†	D1941†	D1987†
D1711	D1758†	D1804†	D1850†	D1896†	D1942†	D1988†
D1712	D1759†	D1805†	D1851†	D1897†	D1943†	D1989†
D1713	D1760†	D1806†	D1852†	D1898†	D1944†	D1990†
D1714	D1761†	D1807†	D1853†	D1899†	D1945†	D1991†
D1715	D1762†	D1808†	D1854†	D1900†	D1946†	D1992†
D1716	D1763†	D1809†	D1855†	D1901†	D1947†	D1993†
D1717	D1764†	D1810†	D1856†	D1902†	D1948†	D1994†
D1718	D1765†	D1811†	D1857†	D1903†	D1949†	D1995†
D1719	D1766†	D1812†	D1858†	D1904†	D1950†	D1996†
D1720	D1767†	D1813†	D1859†	D1905†	D1951†	D1997†
D1721	D1768†	D1814†	D1860†	D1906†	D1952†	D1998†
D1722	D1769†	D1815†	D1861†	D1907†	D1953†	D1999†
D1723	D1770†	D1816†	D1862†	D1908†	D1954†	

TOTAL: 510

Shunter   British Railways   0-6-0

Introduced
1957

Engine
Gardner 8L3 of 204 b.h.p. at 1,200 r.p.m.

Weight
30 tons 16 cwt

Maximum tractive effort
15,650 lb

Total b.h.p.
204

Transmission
Mechanical. Vulcan-Sinclair type 23 fluid coupling. Wilson-Drewry C.A.5 type five-speed epicyclic gearbox. Type RF 11 spiral bevel reverse and final drive unit.

Driving wheel diameter
3′ 7″

* With cut-down cab for working on the BPGV line

D2000	D2029	D2058	D2087	D2116	D2144 *	D2172
D2001	D2030	D2059	D2088	D2117	D2145 *	D2173
D2002	D2031	D2060	D2089	D2118	D2146 *	D2174
D2003	D2032	D2061	D2090	D2119	D2147	D2175
D2004	D2033	D2062	D2091	D2120	D2148	D2176
D2005	D2034	D2063	D2092	D2121	D2149	D2177
D2006	D2035	D2064	D2093	D2122	D2150	D2178
D2007	D2036	D2065	D2094	D2123	D2151	D2179
D2008	D2037	D2066	D2095	D2124	D2152	D2180
D2009	D2038	D2067	D2096	D2125	D2153	D2181
D2010	D2039	D2068	D2097	D2126	D2154	D2182
D2011	D2040	D2069	D2098	D2127	D2155	D2183
D2012	D2041	D2070	D2099	D2128	D2156	D2184
D2013	D2042	D2071	D2100	D2129	D2157	D2185
D2014	D2043	D2072	D2101	D2130	D2158	D2186
D2015	D2044	D2073	D2102	D2131	D2159	D2187
D2016	D2045	D2074	D2103	D2132	D2160	D2188
D2017	D2046	D2075	D2104	D2133 S	D2161	D2189
D2018	D2047	D2076	D2105	D2134	D2162	D2190
D2019	D2048	D2077	D2106	D2135	D2163	D2191
D2020	D2049	D2078	D2107	D2136	D2164	D2192
D2021	D2050	D2079	D2108	D2137	D2165	D2193
D2022	D2051	D2080	D2109	D2138	D2166	D2194
D2023	D2052	D2081	D2110	D2139	D2167	D2195
D2024	D2053	D2082	D2111	D2140	D2168	D2196
D2025	D2054	D2083	D2112	D2141 *	D2169	D2197
D2026	D2055	D2084	D2113	D2142 *	D2170	D2198
D2027	D2056	D2085	D2114	D2143 *	D2171	D2199
D2028	D2057	D2086	D2115 S			

Class continued with D2372

Shunter Drewry 0-6-0

Introduced
1952

Engine
Gardner 8L3 of 204 b.h.p. at 1,200 r.p.m.

Weight
29 tons 15 cwt

Maximum tractive effort
16,850 lb

Total b.h.p.
204

Transmission
Mechanical, Vulcan-Sinclair type 23 fluid coupling. Wilson-Drewry C.A.5 type five-speed epicyclic gearbox. Type RF 11 spiral bevel reverse and final drive unit

Driving wheel diameter
3' 3"

D2200S	D2203S	D2205	D2207S	D2209	D2211	D2213
D2201S	D2204	D2206	D2208	D2210	D2212	D2214
D2202S						

TOTAL: 15

Shunter Drewry 0-6-0

Introduced
1955

Engine
Gardner 8L3 of 204 b.h.p. at 1,200 r.p.m.

Weight
29 tons 15 cwt

Maximum tractive effort
15,650 lb

Total b.h.p.
204

Transmission
Mechanical. Vulcan-Sinclair type 23 fluid coupling. Wilson-Drewry C.A.5 type five-speed epicyclic gearbox. Type RF 11 spiral bevel reverse and final drive unit

Driving wheel diameter
3' 6"

D2215	D2224	D2233	D2242	D2250	D2258	D2266
D2216	D2225	D2234	D2243	D2251	D2259	D2267
D2217	D2226	D2235	D2244	D2252	D2260	D2268
D2218	D2227	D2236S	D2245	D2253	D2261	D2269
D2219	D2228	D2237	D2246		D2262	D2270
D2220	D2229	D2238	D2247	D2255	D2263	D2271
D2221	D2230	D2239	D2248	D2256	D2264	D2272
D2222	D2231	D2240	D2249	D2257	D2265	
D2223	D2232	D2241				

TOTAL: 57

Shunter Drewry 0-6-0

Introduced
1959

Engine
Gardner 8L3 of 204 b.h.p. at 1,200 r.p.m.

Weight
29 tons 15 cwt

Maximum tractive effort
16,850 lb

Total b.h.p.
204

Transmission
Mechanical. Vulcan-Sinclair type 23 fluid coupling. Wilson-Drewry C.A.5 type five-speed epicyclic gearbox. Type RF 11 spiral bevel reverse and final drive unit

Driving wheel diameter
3' 7"

D2274	D2284	D2294	D2304	D2314	D2323	D2332
	D2285	D2295	D2305	D2315	D2324	D2333
D2276	D2286	D2296	D2306	D2316	D2325	D2334
D2277	D2287	D2297	D2307	D2317	D2326	D2335
D2278	D2288	D2298	D2308	D2318	D2327	D2336
D2279	D2289	D2299	D2309	D2319	D2328	D2337
D2280	D2290	D2300	D2310	D2320	D2329	D2338
D2281	D2291	D2301 S	D2311	D2321	D2330	
D2282	D2292	D2302	D2312	D2322	D2331	D2340
D2283	D2293		D2313			

TOTAL: 64

Shunter　　　　　　Drewry　　　　　　0-6-0

Introduced
1947

Engine
Gardner 8L3 of 204 b.h.p.

Weight
24 tons 15 cwt

Maximum tractive effort
16,850 lb

Total b.h.p.
204

Transmission
Mechanical. Five-speed gearbox

Driving wheel diameter
3' 3"

Formerly Departmental locomotive
DS1173

D2341

TOTAL: 1

Shunter　　　　British Railways　　　　0-6-0

Introduced
1958

Engine
Gardner 8L3 of 204 b.h.p. at 1,200
∴p.m.

Weight
30 tons 4 cwt

Maximum tractive effort
15,000 lb

Total b.h.p.
200

Transmission
Mechanical. Wilson-Drewry Director
air-operated epicyclic gearbox. R.F. 11
spiral bevel reverse/final drive unit

Driving wheel diameter
3' 7"

Formerly Departmental locomotives
91 and 92

D2370　　D2371

TOTAL: 2

Shunter　　　　British Railways　　　　0-6-0

Class continued from D2199

D2372	D2376	D2380	D2384	D2388	D2392	D2396
D2373	D2377	D2381	D2385 S	D2389	D2393	D2397
D2374	D2378	D2382	D2386	D2390	D2394	D2398
D2375	D2379	D2383	D2387	D2391	D2395	D2399

TOTAL: 228

British Railways 204 b.h.p. diesel-mechanical 0-6-0 No. D2371
[D. L. Percival

British Railways 204 b.h.p. diesel-mechanical 0-6-0 No. D2377
[D. L. Percival

Barclay 204 b.h.p. diesel - mechanical 0-6-0 No. D2400 (since withdrawn)
[D. L. Percival

Shunter   Barclay   0-6-0

Introduced
1956

Engine
Gardner 8L3 of 204 b.h.p. at 1,200 r.p.m.

Weight
32 tons

Maximum tractive effort
15,340 lb

Total b.h.p.
204

Transmission
Mechanical. Vulcan-Sinclair type 23 fluid coupling. Wilson C.A.4 type four-speed epicyclic gearbox. Wiseman type 15 RLGB reverse and final drive unit

Driving wheel diameter
3′ 6″

D2401	D2403	D2404	D2405	D2407	D2409

TOTAL: 6

Shunter   Barclay   0-4-0

Introduced
1958

Engine
Gardner 8L3 of 204 b.h.p. at 1,200 r.p.m.

Weight
35 tons

Maximum tractive effort
20,000 lb

Total b.h.p.
204

Transmission
Mechanical. Vulcan-Sinclair type 23 fluid coupling. Wilson-Drewry C.A.5 type five-speed epicyclic gearbox. Wiseman type 15 RLGB reverse and final drive unit

Driving wheel diameter
3′ 7″

D2410	D2415	D2420	D2425	D2430	D2435	D2440
D2411	D2416	D2421	D2426	D2431	D2436	
D2412	D2417	D2422	D2427	D2432	D2437	D2442
D2413	D2418	D2423	D2428	D2433	D2438	D2443
D2414	D2419	D2424	D2429	D2434	D2439	D2444

TOTAL: 34

Shunter   Hudswell-Clarke   0-6-0

Introduced
1961

Engine
Gardner 8L3 of 204 b.h.p. at 1,200 r.p.m.

Weight
34 tons 4 cwt

Maximum tractive effort
16,100 lb

Total b.h.p.
204

Transmission
Mechanical. S.C.R.5 type 23 scoop control fluid coupling. Four-speed "SSS Power-flow" double synchro-type gearbox and final drive

Driving wheel diameter
3′ 6″

D2511

TOTAL: 1

Shunter   Hunslet   0-6-0

Introduced
1955

Engine
Gardner 8L3 of 204 b.h.p. at 1,200 r.p.m.

Weight
30 tons

Maximum tractive effort
14,500 lb

Total b.h.p.
204

Transmission
Mechanical. Hunslet patent friction clutch. Hunslet four-speed gearbox incorporating reverse and final drive gears

Driving wheel diameter
3′ 4″
3′ 9″*

D2551	D2571	D2580*	D2589*	D2597*	D2605*	D2611*
D2553	D2573	D2581*	D2590*	D2598*	D2607*	D2613*
D2554	D2574*	D2582*	D2592*	D2599*	D2608*	D2616*
D2555	D2575*	D2583*	D2593*	D2600*	D2609*	D2617*
D2562	D2576*	D2585*	D2595*	D2601*	D2610*	D2618*
D2566	D2579*	D2587*	D2596*	D2604*		

TOTAL: 40

Shunter   North British   0-4-0

Introduced
1953

Engine
Paxman 6RPH of 200 b.h.p. at 1,000 r.p.m.

Weight
32 tons

Maximum tractive effort
21,500 lb

Total b.h.p.
200

Transmission
Hydraulic. Voith-North British hydraulic torque converter type L33YU. North British bevel gears and reversing dog clutch coupled through reduction gearing to jackshaft

Driving wheel diameter
3′ 6″

D2703

TOTAL: 1

Shunter   North British   0-4-0

Introduced
1957

Engine
N.B.L./M.A.N. W6V 17.5/22A of 225 b.h.p. at 1,100 r.p.m. (12 hr rating)

Weight
30 tons

Maximum tractive effort
20,080 lb

Total b.h.p.
225

Transmission
Hydraulic. Voith-North British hydraulic torque converter type LCCYU. North British bevel gears and reversing dog clutch coupled through reduction gearing to jack-shaft

Driving wheel diameter
3′ 6″

D2756	D2760	D2768	D2770	D2775	D2779	D2780
D2758	D2764	D2769	D2773			

TOTAL: 11

Barclay 204 b.h.p. diesel-mechanical 0-4-0 No. D2439   [*P. H. Groom*

Hudswell-Clarke 204
b.h.p. diesel-mech-
anical 0-6-0 No.
D2511
   [*D. L. Percival*

Hunslet 204 b.h.p.
diesel - mechanical
0-6-0 No. D2587
   [*R. A. Panting*

North British 200 b.h.p. diesel-hydraulic 0-4-0 No. D2704 (since withdrawn)
[D. L. Percival

North British 225 b.h.p. diesel-hydraulic 0-4-0 No. D2758   [G. W. Morrison

Shunter   Yorkshire Engine Co.   0-4-0

Introduced
1960

Engine
Rolls-Royce C6NFL of 179 h.p. at
1,800 r.p.m.

Weight
28 tons

Maximum tractive effort
15,000 lb

Total b.h.p.
170

Transmission
Hydraulic. Rolls-Royce 3-stage torque
converter, Series 10,000. Yorkshire
Engine Co. axle-hung double-
reduction final drive with reversing
mechanism

Driving wheel diameter
3′ 6″

D2850	D2853	D2856	D2859	D2862	D2865	D2868
D2851	D2854	D2857	D2860	D2863	D2866	D2869
D2852	D2855	D2858	D2861	D2864	D2867	

TOTAL: 20

Shunter   Hunslet   0-4-0

Introduced
1955

Engine
Gardner 6L3 of 153 b.h.p. at 1,200
r.p.m.

Weight
22 tons 9 cwt

Maximum tractive effort
10,800 lb

Total b.h.p.
153

Transmission
Mechanical. Hunslet patent friction
clutch and four-speed gearbox
incorporating reverse and final
drive gears

Driving wheel diameter
3′ 4″

D2950   D2951

TOTAL: 2

Shunter   Barclay   0-4-0

Introduced
1956

Engine
Gardner 6L3 of 153 b.h.p. at 1,200
r.p.m.

Weight
25 tons

Maximum tractive effort
12,750 lb

Total b.h.p.
153

Transmission
Mechanical. Vulcan-Sinclair rigid type
hydraulic coupling. Wilson S.E. 4
type four-speed epicyclic gearbox.
Wiseman type 15 RLGB reverse and
final drive unit

Driving wheel diameter
3′ 2″

D2954   D2955

TOTAL: 2

Yorkshire Engine Co. 170 b.h.p. diesel-hydraulic 0-4-0 No. D2867
[D. L. Percival]

Hunslet 153 b.h.p. diesel - mechanical 0-4-0 No. D2950
[H. N. James]

Ruston & Hornsby 165 b.h.p. diesel-mechanical 0-4-0 No. D2958
[D. L. Percival]

Shunter   Ruston & Hornsby   0-4-0

Introduced
1956

Engine
Ruston 6VPHL of 165 b.h.p. at 1,250
r.p.m. (1 hr rating)

Weight
28 tons

Maximum tractive effort
14,350 lb

Total b.h.p.
165

Transmission
Mechanical. Oil pressure-operated
S.L.M. type friction clutches incor-
porated in Ruston constant mesh
type gearbox. Reverse gear and final
drive unit incorporating bevel gears
and dog clutches and reduction gear
to final drive

Driving wheel diameter
3' 4"

D2958

TOTAL: 1

Shunter   Ruston & Hornsby   0-6-0

Introduced
1962

Engine
Paxman 6-cyl RPHL

Weight
42 tons 5 cwt

Maximum tractive effort
28,240 lb

Total b.h.p.
275

Transmission
Electric. A.E.I. type RTA 6652 traction
motor, spigot-mounted on a double-
reduction axle-hung final drive
gearbox

Driving wheel diameter
3' 6"

D2985	D2987	D2989	D2991	D2993	D2995	D2997
D2986	D2988	D2990	D2992	D2994	D2996	D2998

TOTAL: 14

Shunter   British Railways   0-6-0

Introduced
1953

Engine
English Electric 6-cyl 6KT of 350
b.h.p. at 630 r.p.m.

Weight
49 tons

Maximum tractive effort
35,000 lb

Total b.h.p.
350

Transmission
Electric. Two English Electric nose-
suspended traction motors. Double
reduction gear drive

Driving wheel diameter
4' 6"

Nos. D3000-91 and D3102-3116 fitted for vacuum brake operation

D3000	D3017	D3034	D3051	D3068 **S**	D3085	D3101
D3001	D3018	D3035	D3052	D3069	D3086	D3102
D3002	D3019	D3036	D3053	D3070	D3087	D3103
D3003	D3020	D3037	D3054	D3071	D3088	D3104
D3004	D3021	D3038	D3055	D3072	D3089	D3105
D3005	D3022	D3039	D3056	D3073	D3090	D3106
D3006	D3023	D3040	D3057	D3074	D3091	D3107
D3007	D3024	D3041	D3058	D3075	D3092	D3108
D3008	D3025	D3042	D3059	D3076	D3093	D3109
D3009	D3026	D3043	D3060	D3077	D3094	D3110
D3010	D3027	D3044	D3061	D3078	D3095	D3111
D3011	D3028	D3045	D3062	D3079	D3096	D3112
D3012	D3029	D3046	D3063	D3080	D3097	D3113
D3013	D3030	D3047	D3064	D3081	D3098	D3114
D3014	D3031	D3048	D3065	D3082	D3099	D3115
D3015	D3032	D3049	D3066	D3083	D3100	D3116
D3016	D3033	D3050	D3067	D3084		

Introduced
1953

Total b.h.p.
350

Engine
English Electric 6-cyl 6KT of 350 b.h.p. at 680 r.p.m.

Transmission
Electric. Two English Electric nose-suspended traction motors. Double reduction gear drive

Weight
48 tons

Driving wheel diameter
4' 6"

Maximum tractive effort
35,000 lb

Fitted for vacuum brake operation

| D3127 | D3129 | D3131 | D3133 | D3134 | D3135 | D3136 |
| D3128 | D3130 | D3132 | | | | |

Introduced
1955

Total b.h.p.
350

Engine
Blackstone 6-cyl ER6T of 350 b.h.p. at 750 r.p.m.

Transmission
Electric. Two G.E.C. nose-suspended traction motors. Double reduction gear drive

Weight
47 tons 10 cwt

Driving wheel diameter
4' 6"

Maximum tractive effort
35,000 lb

Fitted for vacuum brake operation

D3137	D3140	D3142	D3144	D3146	D3148	D3150
D3138	D3141	D3143	D3145	D3147	D3149	D3151
D3139						

Top: Ruston & Hornsby 275 b.h.p. diesel-electric 0-6-0 No. D2998.
[H. Luff/OTA]

Centre: British Railways 350 b.h.p. diesel-electric 0-6-0 No. D3266
[D. L. Percival]

Right: British Railways 350 b.h.p. diesel-electric 0-6-0 No. D3464 (in blue livery)
[A. D. McIntyre]

77

D3167	D3206	D3245	D3284	D3323	D3362	D3401
D3168	D3207	D3246	D3285	D3324	D3363	D3402
D3169	D3208	D3247	D3286	D3325	D3364	D3403
D3170	D3209	D3248	D3287	D3326	D3365	D3404
D3171	D3210	D3249	D3288	D3327	D3366	D3405
D3172	D3211	D3250	D3289	D3328	D3367	D3406
D3173	D3212	D3251	D3290	D3329	D3368	D3407
D3174	D3213	D3252	D3291	D3330	D3369	D3408
D3175	D3214	D3253	D3292	D3331	D3370	D3409
D3176	D3215	D3254	D3293	D3332	D3371	D3410
D3177	D3216	D3255	D3294	D3333	D3372	D3411
D3178	D3217	D3256	D3295	D3334	D3373	D3412
D3179	D3218	D3257	D3296	D3335	D3374	D3413
D3180	D3219	D3258	D3297	D3336	D3375	D3414
D3181	D3220	D3259	D3298	D3337	D3376	D3415
D3182	D3221	D3260	D3299	D3338	D3377	D3416
D3183	D3222	D3261	D3300	D3339	D3378	D3417
D3184	D3223	D3262	D3301	D3340	D3379	D3418
D3185	D3224	D3263	D3302	D3341	D3380	D3419
D3186	D3225	D3264	D3303	D3342	D3381	D3420
D3187	D3226	D3265	D3304	D3343	D3382	D3421
D3188	D3227	D3266	D3305	D3344	D3383	D3422
D3189	D3228 S	D3267	D3306	D3345	D3384	D3423
D3190	D3229	D3268	D3307	D3346	D3385	D3424
D3191	D3230	D3269	D3308	D3347	D3386	D3425
D3192	D3231	D3270	D3309	D3348	D3387	D3426
	D3232	D3271	D3310	D3349	D3388	D3427
D3194	D3233	D3272	D3311	D3350	D3389	D3428
D3195	D3234	D3273	D3312	D3351	D3390	D3429
D3196	D3235	D3274	D3313	D3352	D3391	D3430
D3197	D3236	D3275	D3314	D3353	D3392	D3431
D3198	D3237	D3276	D3315	D3354	D3393	D3432
D3199	D3238	D3277	D3316	D3355	D3394	D3433
D3200	D3239	D3278	D3317	D3356	D3395	D3434
D3201	D3240	D3279	D3318	D3357	D3396	D3435
D3202	D3241	D3280	D3319	D3358	D3397	D3436
D3203	D3242	D3281	D3320	D3359	D3398	D3437
D3204	D3243	D3282	D3321	D3360	D3399	D3438
D3205	D3244	D3283	D3322	D3361	D3400	

D3439	D3442	D3444	D3446	D3448	D3450	D3452
D3440	D3443	D3445	D3447	D3449	D3451	D3453
D3441						

D3454-D3472: for particulars see D3127-D3136

D3454	D3457	D3460	D3463	D3466	D3469	D3471
D3455	D3458	D3461	D3464	D3467	D3470	D3472
D3456	D3459	D3462	D3465	D3468		

D3473-D3502: for particulars see D3137-D3151

D3473	D3478	D3483	D3487	D3491	D3495	D3499
D3474	D3479	D3484	D3488	D3492		D3500
D3475	D3480	D3485	D3489	D3493	D3497	D3501
D3476	D3481	D3486	D3490	D3494	D3498	D3502
D3477	D3482					

D3503-D3611: for particulars see D3127-D3136

D3503	D3519	D3535	D3551	D3567	D3582	D3597
D3504	D3520	D3536	D3552	D3568	D3583	D3598
D3505	D3521	D3537	D3553	D3569	D3584	D3599
D3506	D3522	D3538	D3554	D3570	D3585	D3600
D3507	D3523	D3539	D3555	D3571	D3586	D3601
D3508	D3524	D3540	D3556	D3572	D3587	D3602
D3509	D3525	D3541	D3557	D3573	D3588	D3603
D3510	D3526	D3542	D3558	D3574	D3589	D3604
D3511	D3527	D3543	D3559	D3575	D3590	D3605
D3512	D3528	D3544	D3560	D3576	D3591	D3606
D3513	D3529	D3545	D3561	D3577	D3592	D3607
D3514	D3530	D3546	D3562	D3578	D3593	D3608
D3515	D3531	D3547	D3563	D3579	D3594	D3609
D3516	D3532	D3548	D3564	D3580	D3595	D3610
D3517	D3533	D3549	D3565	D3581	D3596	D3611
D3518	D3534	D3550	D3566			

D3612-D3651: for particulars see D3137-D3151

D3612	D3618	D3624	D3630	D3636	D3642	D3647
D3613	D3619	D3625		D3637	D3643	D3648
D3614		D3626	D3632	D3638	D3644	D3649
D3615	D3621	D3627	D3633	D3639	D3645	D3650
D3616	D3622	D3628	D3634	D3640	D3646	D3651
D3617	D3623	D3629	D3635	D3641		

D3652-D4048: for particulars see D3127-D3136

D3652	D3658	D3664	D3670	D3676	D3682	D3688
D3653	D3659	D3665	D3671	D3677	D3683	D3689
D3654	D3660	D3666	D3672	D3678	D3684	D3690
D3655	D3661	D3667	D3673	D3679	D3685	D3691
D3656	D3662	D3668	D3674	D3680	D3686	D3692
D3657	D3663	D3669	D3675	D3681	D3687	D3693

D3694	D3744	D3792	D3840	D3888	D3936	D3984
D3695	D3745	D3793	D3841	D3889	D3937	D3985
D3696	D3746	D3794	D3842	D3890	D3938	D3986
D3699	D3747	D3795	D3843	D3891	D3939	D3987
D3700	D3748	D3796	D3844	D3892	D3940	D3988
D3701	D3749	D3797	D3845	D3893	D3941	D3989
D3702	D3750	D3798	D3846	D3894	D3942	D3990
D3703	D3751	D3799	D3847	D3895	D3943	D3991
D3704	D3752	D3800	D3848	D3896	D3944	D3992
D3705	D3753	D3801	D3849	D3897	D3945	D3993
D3706	D3754	D3802	D3850	D3898	D3946	D3994
D3707	D3755	D3803	D3851	D3899	D3947	D3995
D3708	D3756	D3804	D3852	D3900	D3948	D3996
D3709	D3757	D3805	D3853	D3901	D3949	D3997
D3710	D3758	D3806	D3854	D3902	D3950	D3998
D3711	D3759	D3807	D3855	D3903	D3951	D3999
D3712	D3760	D3808	D3856	D3904	D3952	D4000
D3713	D3761	D3809	D3857	D3905	D3953	D4001
D3714	D3762	D3810	D3858	D3906	D3954	D4002
D3715	D3763	D3811	D3859	D3907	D3955	D4003
D3716	D3764	D3812	D3860	D3908	D3956	D4004
D3717	D3765	D3813	D3861	D3909	D3957	D4005
D3718	D3766	D3814	D3862	D3910	D3958	D4006
D3719	D3767	D3815	D3863	D3911	D3959	D4007
D3720	D3768	D3816	D3864	D3912	D3960	D4008
D3721	D3769	D3817	D3865	D3913	D3961	D4009
D3722	D3770	D3818	D3866	D3914	D3962	D4010
D3723	D3771	D3819	D3867	D3915	D3963	D4011
D3724	D3772	D3820	D3868	D3916	D3964	D4012
D3725	D3773	D3821	D3869	D3917	D3965	D4013
D3726	D3774	D3822	D3870	D3918	D3966	D4014
D3727	D3775	D3823	D3871	D3919	D3967	D4015
D3728	D3776	D3824	D3872	D3920	D3968	D4016
D3729	D3777	D3825	D3873	D3921	D3969	D4017
D3730	D3778	D3826	D3874	D3922	D3970	D4018
D3731	D3779	D3827	D3875	D3923	D3971	D4019
D3732	D3780	D3828	D3876	D3924	D3972	D4020
D3733	D3781	D3829	D3877	D3925	D3973	D4021
D3734	D3782	D3830	D3878	D3926	D3974	D4022
D3735	D3783	D3831	D3879	D3927	D3975	D4023
D3736	D3784	D3832	D3880	D3928	D3976	D4024
D3737	D3785	D3833	D3881	D3929	D3977	D4025
D3738	D3786	D3834	D3882	D3930	D3978	D4026
D3739	D3787	D3835	D3883	D3931	D3979	D4027
D3740	D3788	D3836	D3884	D3932	D3980	D4028
D3741	D3789	D3837	D3885	D3933	D3981	D4029
D3742	D3790	D3838	D3886	D3934	D3982	D4030
D3743	D3791	D3839	D3887	D3935	D3983	D4031

D4032	D4035	D4038	D4041	D4043	D4045	D4047
D4033	D4036	D4039	D4042	D4044	D4046	D4048
D4034	D4037	D4040				

D4049-D4094: for particulars see D3137-D3151

D4049	D4056	D4063	D4070	D4077	D4083	D4089
D4050	D4057	D4064	D4071	D4078	D4084	D4090
D4051	D4058	D4065	D4072	D4079	D4085	D4091
D4052	D4059	D4066	D4073	D4080	D4086	D4092
D4053	D4060	D4067	D4074	D4081	D4087	D4093
D4054	D4061	D4068	D4075	D4082	D4088	D4094
D4055	D4062	D4069	D4076			

D4095-D4192: for particulars see D3127-D3136

D4095	D4109	D4123	D4137	D4150	D4163	D4176
D4096	D4110	D4124	D4138	D4151	D4164	D4177
D4097	D4111	D4125	D4139	D4152	D4165	D4178
D4098	D4112	D4126	D4140	D4153	D4166	D4179
D4099	D4113	D4127	D4141	D4154	D4167	D4180
D4100	D4114	D4128	D4142	D4155	D4168	D4181
D4101	D4115	D4129	D4143	D4156	D4169	D4182
D4102	D4116	D4130	D4144	D4157	D4170	D4183
D4103	D4117	D4131	D4145	D4158	D4171	D4184
D4104	D4118	D4132	D4146	D4159	D4172	D4185
D4105	D4119	D4133	D4147	D4160	D4173	D4186
D4106	D4120	D4134	D4148	D4161	D4174	D4191
D4107	D4121	D4135	D4149	D4162	D4175	D4192
D4108	D4122	D4136				

TOTAL: 1158

Shunter   British Railways   0-6-0-0-6-0

Permanently coupled "master" and "slave*" units, converted from standard 0-6-0 diesels for hump shunting in Tinsley Yard. The cab of the "slave" unit has been removed and both units are specially weighted.

Introduced
1965

Engine
Two English Electric 6-cyl 6KT of 350 b.h.p. at 680 r.p.m.

Weight
120 tons

Maximum tractive effort
70,000 lb

Total b.h.p.
700

Transmission
Electric. Four English Electric nose-suspended traction motors. Double reduction gear drive

Driving wheel diameter
4' 6"

(Original numbers in brackets)

| D4500 | (D3698*, | D4188) | | D4502 | (D3697*, | D4187) |
| D4501 | (D4189*, | D4190) | | | | |

TOTAL: 3

British Railways Type 2 1,160 b.h.p. diesel-electric Bo-Bo No. D5023 [*D. L. Percival*

British Railways Type 2 1,250 b.h.p. diesel-electric Bo-Bo No. D5159 [*D. L. Percival*

British Railways Type 2 1,250 b.h.p. diesel-electric Bo-Bo No. D5253 [*D. L. Percival*

Type 2   British Railways   Bo-Bo

Introduced
1958

Engine
Sulzer 6-cyl 6LDA28 of 1,160 b.h.p.
at 750 r.p.m.
†‡Sulzer 6-cyl 6LDA28-B of 1,250
b.h.p. at 750 r.p.m.

Weight
75 tons
72 tons 17 cwt*†

Maximum tractive effort
40,000 lb
‡45,000 lb

Total b.h.p.   ★
1,160
1,160*
1,250†‡§

Transmission
Electric. Four B.T.H. axle-hung,
nose-suspended traction motors of
213 h.p. (continuous rating)
‡§Four A.E.I. 253 AY nose-suspended
traction motors

Driving wheel diameter
3' 9"

D5000	D5035	D5070	D5105*	D5140*	D5175†	D5210‡
D5001	D5036	D5071	D5106*	D5141*	D5176‡	D5211‡
D5002	D5037	D5072	D5107*	D5142*	D5177‡	D5212‡
D5003	D5038	D5073	D5108*	D5143*	D5178‡	D5213‡
D5004	D5039	D5074	D5109*	D5144*	D5179‡	D5214‡
D5005	D5040	D5075	D5110*	D5145*	D5180‡	D5215‡
D5006	D5041	D5076	D5111*	D5146*	D5181‡	D5216‡
D5007	D5042	D5077	D5112*	D5147*	D5182‡	D5217‡
D5008	D5043	D5078	D5113*	D5148*	D5183‡	D5218‡
D5009	D5044	D5079	D5114*	D5149*	D5184‡	D5219‡
D5010	D5045	D5080	D5115*	D5150*	D5185‡	D5220‡
D5011	D5046	D5081	D5116*	D5151†	D5186‡	D5221‡
D5012	D5047	D5082	D5117*	D5152†	D5187‡	D5222‡
D5013	D5048	D5083	D5118*	D5153†	D5188‡	D5223‡
D5014	D5049	D5084	D5119*	D5154†	D5189‡	D5224‡
D5015	D5050	D5085	D5120*	D5155†	D5190‡	D5225‡
D5016		D5086	D5121*	D5156†	D5191‡	D5226‡
D5017	D5052	D5087	D5122*	D5157†	D5192‡	D5227‡
D5018	D5053	D5088	D5123*	D5158†	D5193‡	D5228‡
D5019	D5054	D5089	D5124*	D5159†	D5194‡	D5229‡
D5020	D5055	D5090	D5125*	D5160†	D5195‡	D5230‡
D5021	D5056	D5091	D5126*	D5161†	D5196‡	D5231‡
D5022	D5057	D5092	D5127*	D5162†	D5197‡	D5232‡
D5023	D5058	D5093	D5128*	D5163†	D5198‡	D5233§
D5024	D5059	D5094*	D5129*	D5164†	D5199‡	D5234§
D5025	D5060	D5095*	D5130*	D5165†	D5200‡	D5235§
D5026	D5061	D5096*	D5131*	D5166†	D5201‡	D5236§
D5027	D5062	D5097*	D5132*	D5167†	D5202‡	D5237§
D5028	D5063	D5098*	D5133*	D5168†	D5203‡	D5238§
D5029	D5064	D5099*	D5134*	D5169†	D5204‡	D5239§
D5030	D5065	D5100*	D5135*	D5170†	D5205‡	D5240§
D5031	D5066	D5101*	D5136*	D5171†	D5206‡	D5241§
D5032	D5067	D5102*	D5137*	D5172†	D5207‡	D5242§
D5033	D5068	D5103*	D5138*	D5173†	D5208‡	D5243§
D5034	D5069	D5104*	D5139*	D5174†	D5209‡	D5244§

Birmingham R.C. & W. Co. Type 2 1,160 b.h.p. diesel-electric Bo-Bo No. D5306
[L. Booth

Birmingham R.C. & W. Co. Type 2 1,250 b.h.p. diesel-electric Bo-Bo No. D5360
[D. J. Dippie

Brush Type 2 1,470 b.h.p. diesel-electric A1A-A1A No. D5562   [D. L. Percival

D5245§	D5253§	D5261§	D5269§	D5277§	D5285§	D5293§
D5246§	D5254§	D5262§	D5270§	D5278§	D5286§	D5294§
D5247§	D5255§	D5263§	D5271§	D5279§	D5287§	D5295§
D5248§	D5256§	D5264§	D5272§	D5280§	D5288§	D5296§
D5249§	D5257§	D5265§	D5273§	D5281§	D5289§	D5297§
D5250§	D5258§	D5266§	D5274§	D5282§	D5290§	D5298§
D5251§	D5259§	D5267§	D5275§	D5283§	D5291§	D5299§
D5252§	D5260§	D5268§	D5276§	D5284§	D5292§	

Class continued with D7500

Type 2   Birmingham   Bo-Bo
R.C. & W. Co.

Introduced
1958

Engine
Sulzer 6-cyl 6LDA28 of 1,160 b.h.p.
at 750 r.p.m.
† Sulzer 6-cyl 6LDA28-B of 1,250
b.h.p. at 750 r.p.m.

Weight
74 tons
77 tons 10 cwt*
72 tons 10 cwt†

Maximum tractive effort
42,000 lb

Total b.h.p.   ★
1,160
1,250†

Transmission
Electric. Four Crompton Parkinson
axle-hung, nose-suspended traction
motors
†Four G.E.C. axle-hung, nose-
suspended traction motors

Driving wheel diameter
3′ 7″

D5300*	D5317*	D5334	D5351†	D5367†	D5384†	D5400†
D5301*	D5318*	D5335	D5352†	D5368†	D5385†	D5401†
D5302*	D5319*	D5336	D5353†	D5369†	D5386†	D5402†
D5303*	D5320	D5337	D5354†	D5370†	D5387†	D5403†
D5304*	D5321	D5338	D5355†	D5371†	D5388†	D5404†
D5305*	D5322	D5339	D5356†	D5372†	D5389†	D5405†
D5306*	D5323	D5340	D5357†	D5373†	D5390†	D5406†
D5307*	D5324	D5341	D5358†	D5374†	D5391†	D5407†
D5308*	D5325	D5342	D5359†	D5375†	D5392†	D5408†
D5309*	D5326	D5343	D5360†	D5376†	D5393†	D5409†
D5310*	D5327	D5344	D5361†	D5377†	D5394†	D5410†
D5311*	D5328	D5345	D5362†	D5378†	D5395†	D5411†
D5312*	D5329	D5346	D5363†	D5379†	D5396†	D5412†
D5313*	D5330	D5347†	D5364†	D5380†	D5397†	D5413†
D5314*	D5331	D5348†	D5365†	D5381†	D5398†	D5414†
D5315*	D5332	D5349†	D5366†	D5382†	D5399†	D5415†
D5316*	D5333	D5350†				

TOTAL: 115

Type 2 or 3†   Brush   A1A-A1A

Introduced
1957

Engine
Mirrlees, Bickerton & Day 12-cyl JVS12T of 1,250 b.h.p. at 850 r.p.m.
†Temporarily uprated to 1,600 b.h.p.
‡ English Electric 12-cyl 12SV of 1,470 b.h.p.

Weight
104 tons

Maximum tractive effort
42,000 lb

Total b.h.p.   ●* ★
1,250
1,600†
1,470‡

Transmission
Electric. Four Brush traction motors. single reduction gear drive

Driving wheel diameter
3′ 7″

D5500*	D5529	D5558	D5587‡	D5616‡	D5644‡	D5672
D5501*	D5530	D5559‡	D5588‡	D5617‡	D5645‡	D5673‡
D5502*	D5531	D5560	D5589	D5618‡	D5646‡	D5674‡
D5503*	D5532‡	D5561‡	D5590‡	D5619	D5647‡	D5675‡
D5504*	D5533	D5562‡	D5591‡	D5620‡	D5648‡	D5676‡
D5505*	D5534‡	D5563	D5592	D5621	D5649‡	D5677‡
D5506*	D5535	D5564	D5593‡	D5622‡	D5650‡	D5678‡
D5507*	D5536‡	D5565	D5594‡	D5623‡	D5651‡	D5679
D5508*	D5537‡	D5566‡	D5595‡	D5624‡	D5652	D5680‡
D5509*	D5538	D5567	D5596‡	D5625‡	D5653‡	D5681‡
D5510*	D5539	D5568‡	D5597‡	D5626‡	D5654‡	D5682
D5511*	D5540‡	D5569‡	D5598‡	D5627‡	D5655	D5683‡
D5512*	D5541‡	D5570‡	D5599	D5628‡	D5656	D5684‡
D5513*	D5542	D5571‡	D5600‡	D5629	D5657	D5685‡
D5514*	D5543	D5572	D5601‡	D5630‡	D5658‡	D5686‡
D5515*	D5544	D5573	D5602‡	D5631‡	D5659	D5687‡
D5516*	D5545	D5574‡	D5603‡	D5632‡	D5660‡	D5688‡
D5517*	D5546‡	D5575	D5604‡	D5633‡	D5661	D5689‡
D5518‡	D5547	D5576‡	D5605‡	D5634	D5662‡	D5690‡
D5519‡	D5548‡	D5577	D5606‡	D5635‡	D5663‡	D5691‡
D5520‡	D5549‡	D5578	D5607‡	D5636‡	D5664‡	D5692‡
D5521‡	D5550	D5579	D5608‡	D5637‡	D5665‡	D5693‡
D5522‡	D5551‡	D5580‡	D5609‡	D5638‡	D5666‡	D5694‡
D5523‡	D5552	D5581‡	D5610‡	D5639	D5667‡	D5695
D5524‡	D5553‡	D5582	D5611‡	D5640‡	D5668‡	D5696‡
D5525‡	D5554	D5583	D5612‡	D5641	D5669	D5697‡
D5526	D5555‡	D5584‡	D5613‡	D5642‡	D5670	D5698‡
D5527‡	D5556‡	D5585‡	D5614‡	D5643‡	D5671‡	D5699‡
D5528	D5557‡	D5586‡	D5615			

Class continued with D5800

Token exchange apparatus fitted to Brush Type 2 1,250 b.h.p. diesel-electric AIA-AIA
No. D5672 [D. L. Percival

Brush Type 2 1,470 b.h.p. diesel-electric AIA-AIA No. D5692 [D. L. Percival

Metropolitan Vickers Type 2 1,200 b.h.p. diesel-electric Co-Bo No. D5716
[D. L. Percival

Type 2   Metropolitan   Co-Bo
                                Vickers
                                                                    ●

Introduced
1958

Engine
Crossley 8-cyl HST V8 of 1,200
b.h.p. at 625 r.p.m. (continuous)

Weight
97 tons

Maximum tractive effort
50,000 lb

Total b.h.p.
1,200

Transmission
Electric. Five Metropolitan-Vickers
axle-hung nose-suspended traction
motors

Driving wheel diameter
3' 3½"

D5700	D5703	D5706	D5709	D5712	D5715	D5718
D5701	D5704	D5707	D5710	D5713	D5716	D5719
D5702	D5705	D5708	D5711	D5714	D5717	

TOTAL: 20

Type 2 or 3†   Brush   A1A-A1A

Class continued from D5699   ★

D5800‡	D5809‡	D5818‡	D5827‡	D5836	D5845‡	D5854‡
D5801‡	D5810‡	D5819‡	D5828‡	D5837‡	D5846‡	D5855‡
D5802‡	D5811‡	D5820‡	D5829‡	D5838‡	D5847‡	D5856‡
D5803‡	D5812‡	D5821‡	D5830‡	D5839	D5848‡	D5857‡
D5804‡	D5813‡	D5822‡	D5831‡	D5840‡	D5849‡	D5858‡
D5805‡	D5814‡	D5823‡	D5832‡	D5841‡	D5850‡	D5859‡
D5806‡	D5815‡	D5824‡	D5833‡	D5842‡	D5851	D5860
D5807‡	D5816‡	D5825‡	D5834‡	D5843‡	D5852‡	D5861‡
D5808‡	D5817‡	D5826‡	D5835†	D5844‡	D5853	D5862‡

TOTAL: 263

Type 2   English Electric   Bo-Bo

Introduced
1959

Engine
Napier 9-cyl "Deltic" T9-29 two-
stroke, pressure-charged, of 1,100
b.h.p. at 1,600 r.p.m.

Weight
73 tons 17 cwt

Maximum tractive effort
47,000 lb

Total b.h.p.
1,100   ★

Transmission
Electric. Four English Electric axle-
hung nose-suspended traction motors

Driving wheel diameter
3' 7"

D5900	D5902	D5904	D5906	D5907	D5908	D5909
D5901	D5903	D5905				

TOTAL: 10

English Electric Type 2 1,100 b.h.p. diesel-electric Bo-Bo No. D5906 [*D. L. Percival*

North British Type 2 1,350 b.h.p. diesel-electric Bo-Bo No. D6114 [*D. L. Percival*

North British Type 2 1,000 b.h.p. diesel-electric Bo-Bo No. D6115 [*N. E. Preedy*

Type 2 North British Bo-Bo

Introduced
1959

Engine
N.B.L./M.A.N. 12-cyl L12V18/21S, pressure-charged, of 1,000 or 1,100* b.h.p.
†Paxman

Weight
72 tons 10 cwt

Maximum tractive effort
45,000 lb

Total b.h.p.
1,000
1,100*
1,350†

● ★ •

Transmission
Electric. Four G.E.C. nose-suspended traction motors

Driving wheel diameter
3′ 7″

D6100	D6109	D6118	D6126	D6134	D6142*	D6150*
D6101†	D6110	D6119	D6127	D6135*	D6143*	D6151*
D6102†	D6111	D6120	D6128	D6136	D6144*	D6152*
D6103†	D6112†	D6121†	D6129†	D6137†	D6145*	D6153*
D6104*	D6113†	D6122*	D6130†	D6138*	D6146*	D6154*
D6105	D6114†	D6123†	D6131	D6139*	D6147*	D6155*
D6106†	D6115	D6124	D6132†	D6140*	D6148*	D6156*
D6107†	D6116†	D6125	D6133†	D6141*	D6149*	D6157*
D6108	D6117					

TOTAL: 58

Type 2 North British B-B

Introduced
1959

Engine
N.B.L./M.A.N. 12-cyl L12V18/21M of 1,000* or 1,100 b.h.p.

Weight
68 tons*
65 tons

Maximum tractive effort
40,000 lb

Total b.h.p.
1,000*
1,100

□* ◇

Transmission
Hydraulic. Voith-N.B.L. L.T.306r hydraulic transmission and cardan shafts to primary gear-boxes on the inner axles and secondary gear-boxes on the outer axles

Driving wheel diameter
3′ 7″

D6300*	D6309	D6318	D6326	D6334	D6342	D6350
D6301*	D6310	D6319	D6327	D6335	D6343	D6351
D6302*	D6311	D6320	D6328	D6336	D6344	D6352
D6303*	D6312	D6321	D6329	D6337	D6345	D6353
D6304*	D6313	D6322	D6330	D6338	D6346	D6354
D6305*	D6314	D6323	D6331	D6339	D6347	D6355
D6306	D6315	D6324	D6332	D6340	D6348	D6356
D6307	D6316	D6325	D6333	D6341	D6349	D6357
D6308	D6317					

TOTAL: 58

North British Type 2 1,000 b.h.p. diesel-hydraulic B-B No. D6301 [*D. L. Percival*

North British Type 2 1,100 b.h.p. diesel-hydraulic B-B No. D6314 (in blue livery)
[*D. L. Percival*

Birmingham R.C. & W. Co. Type 3 1,550 b.h.p. diesel-electric Bo-Bo No. D6500
[*D. L. Percival*

Type 3   Birmingham   Bo-Bo
R.C. & W. Co. ★

Introduced
1960

Engine
Sulzer 8-cyl 8LDA28 pressure-charged of 1,550 b.h.p. at 750 r.p.m. (continuous)

Weight
73 tons 8 cwt

Maximum tractive effort
45,000 lb

Total b.h.p.
1,550

Transmission
Electric. Four Crompton Parkinson 305 h.p. axle-hung nose-suspended traction motors

Driving wheel diameter
3' 7"

*Built to Hastings line gauge

† Fitted with train air brake equipment and multiple-unit control apparatus

D6500	D6515	D6529†	D6543	D6557	D6571	D6585
D6501	D6516†	D6530	D6544	D6558	D6572	D6586*
D6503	D6517†	D6531†	D6545	D6559	D6573	D6587*
D6504	D6518	D6532†	D6546	D6560	D6574	D6588*
D6505	D6519†	D6533†	D6547	D6561	D6575	D6589*
D6506	D6520†	D6534	D6548	D6562	D6576	D6590*
D6507	D6521†	D6535†	D6549	D6563	D6577	D6591*
D6508	D6522	D6536†	D6550	D6564	D6578	D6592*
D6509	D6523	D6537	D6551	D6565	D6579	D6593*
D6510	D6524	D6538†	D6552	D6566	D6580†	D6594*
D6511†	D6525†	D6539	D6553	D6567	D6581	D6595*
D6512	D6526	D6540	D6554	D6568	D6582	D6596*
D6513†	D6527†	D6541	D6555	D6569	D6583	D6597*
D6514†	D6528†	D6542	D6556	D6570	D6584	

TOTAL: 97

Type 3   English Electric   Co-Co ★

Introduced
1961

Engine
English Electric 12-cyl 12CSVT of 1,750 b.h.p. at 850 r.p.m.

Weight
108 tons

Maximum tractive effort
55,500 lb

Total b.h.p.
1,750

Transmission
Electric. Six English Electric axle-hung nose-suspended traction motors

Driving wheel diameter
3' 7"

* Fitted with train air brake equipment

D6600	D6701	D6711	D6721	D6731	D6741	D6751
D6601	D6702	D6712	D6722	D6732	D6742	D6752
D6602	D6703	D6713	D6723	D6733	D6743	D6753
D6603	D6704	D6714	D6724	D6734	D6744	D6754
D6604	D6705	D6715	D6725	D6735	D6745	D6755
D6605	D6706	D6716	D6726	D6736	D6746	D6756
D6606	D6707	D6717	D6727	D6737	D6747	D6757
D6607	D6708	D6718	D6728	D6738	D6748	D6758
D6608	D6709	D6719	D6729	D6739	D6749	D6759
D6700	D6710	D6720	D6730	D6740	D6750	D6760

93

D6761	D6796	D6830	D6864	D6898	D6932	D6966 *
D6762	D6797	D6831	D6865	D6899	D6933	D6967 *
D6763	D6798	D6832	D6866	D6900	D6934	D6968 *
D6764	D6799	D6833	D6867	D6901	D6935	D6969
D6765	D6800	D6834	D6868	D6902	D6936	D6970
D6766	D6801	D6835	D6869	D6903	D6937	D6971
D6767	D6802	D6836	D6870	D6904	D6938	D6972
D6768	D6803	D6837	D6871	D6905	D6939	D6973
D6769	D6804	D6838	D6872	D6906	D6940	D6974
D6770	D6805	D6839	D6873	D6907	D6941	D6975
D6771	D6806	D6840	D6874	D6908	D6942	D6976
D6772	D6807	D6841	D6875	D6909	D6943	D6977
D6773	D6808	D6842	D6876	D6910	D6944	D6978
D6774	D6809	D6843	D6877	D6911	D6945	D6979
D6775	D6810	D6844	D6878	D6912	D6946	D6980
D6776	D6811	D6845	D6879	D6913	D6947	D6981
D6777	D6812	D6846	D6880	D6914	D6948	D6982
D6778	D6813	D6847	D6881	D6915	D6949	
D6779	D6814	D6848	D6882	D6916	D6950	D6984
D6780	D6815	D6849	D6883	D6917	D6951	D6985
D6781	D6816	D6850	D6884	D6918	D6952	D6986
D6782	D6817	D6851	D6885	D6919	D6953	D6987
D6783	D6818	D6852	D6886	D6920	D6954	D6988
D6784	D6819	D6853	D6887	D6921	D6955	D6989
D6785	D6820	D6854	D6888	D6922	D6956	D6990
D6786	D6821	D6855	D6889	D6923	D6957	D6991
D6787	D6822	D6856	D6890	D6924	D6958	D6992
D6788	D6823	D6857	D6891	D6925	D6959 *	D6993
D6789	D6824	D6858	D6892	D6926	D6960 *	D6994
D6790	D6825	D6859	D6893	D6927	D6961 *	D6995
D6791	D6826	D6860	D6894	D6928	D6962 *	D6996
D6792	D6827	D6861	D6895	D6929	D6963 *	D6997
D6793	D6828	D6862	D6896	D6930	D6964 *	D6998
D6794	D6829	D6863	D6897	D6931	D6965 *	D6999
D6795						

TOTAL: 308

Type 3   Beyer Peacock (Hymek)   B-B

Introduced
1961

Total b.h.p.
1,700   △

Engine
Bristol-Siddeley/Maybach MD870 of
1,700 b.h.p.

Transmission
Hydraulic. Stone-Maybach Mekydro
type 6184U

Weight
74 tons

Driving wheel diameter
3' 9"

Maximum tractive effort
49,700 lb

Beyer-Peacock (Hymek) Type 3 1,700 b.h.p. diesel-hydraulic B-B No. D7004 (in blue livery)
[P. J. Fowler

Beyer-Peacock (Hymek) Type 3 1,700 b.h.p. diesel-hydraulic B-B No. D7080
[D. L. Percival

British Railways Type 2 1,250 b.h.p. diesel-electric Bo-Bo No. D7667 (in blue livery)
[British Railways

95

D7000	D7015	D7030	D7045	D7059	D7073	D7087
D7001	D7016	D7031	D7046	D7060	D7074	D7088
D7002	D7017	D7032	D7047	D7061	D7075	D7089
D7003	D7018	D7033	D7048	D7062	D7076	D7090
D7004	D7019	D7034	D7049	D7063	D7077	D7091
D7005	D7020	D7035	D7050	D7064	D7078	D7092
D7006	D7021	D7036	D7051	D7065	D7079	D7093
D7007	D7022	D7037	D7052	D7066	D7080	D7094
D7008	D7023	D7038	D7053	D7067	D7081	D7095
D7009	D7024	D7039	D7054	D7068	D7082	D7096
D7010	D7025	D7040	D7055	D7069	D7083	D7097
D7011	D7026	D7041	D7056	D7070	D7084	D7098
D7012	D7027	D7042	D7057	D7071	D7085	D7099
D7013	D7028	D7043	D7058	D7072	D7086	D7100
D7014	D7029	D7044				

TOTAL: 101

Type 2   British Railways   Bo-Bo

★

Class continued from D5299

D7500§	D7526§	D7552§	D7578§	D7603§	D7628§	D7653§
D7501§	D7527§	D7553§	D7579§	D7604§	D7629§	D7654§
D7502§	D7528§	D7554§	D7580§	D7605§	D7630§	D7655§
D7503§	D7529§	D7555§	D7581§	D7606§	D7631§	D7656§
D7504§	D7530§	D7556§	D7582§	D7607§	D7632§	D7657§
D7505§	D7531§	D7557§	D7583§	D7608§	D7633§	D7658§
D7506§	D7532§	D7558§	D7584§	D7609§	D7634§	D7659§
D7507§	D7533§	D7559§	D7585§	D7610§	D7635§	D7660§
D7508§	D7534§	D7560§	D7586§	D7611§	D7636§	D7661§
D7509§	D7535§	D7561§	D7587§	D7612§	D7637§	D7662§
D7510§	D7536§	D7562§	D7588§	D7613§	D7638§	D7663§
D7511§	D7537§	D7563§	D7589§	D7614§	D7639§	D7664§
D7512§	D7538§	D7564§	D7590§	D7615§	D7640§	D7665§
D7513§	D7539§	D7565§	D7591§	D7616§	D7641§	D7666§
D7514§	D7540§	D7566§	D7592§	D7617§	D7642§	D7667§
D7515§	D7541§	D7567§	D7593§	D7618§	D7643§	D7668§
D7516§	D7542§	D7568§	D7594§	D7619§	D7644§	D7669§
D7517§	D7543§	D7569§	D7595§	D7620§	D7645§	D7670§
D7518§	D7544§	D7570§	D7596§	D7621§	D7646§	D7671§
D7519§	D7545§	D7571§	D7597§	D7622§	D7647§	D7672§
D7520§	D7546§	D7572§	D7598§	D7623§	D7648§	D7673§
D7521§	D7547§	D7573§	D7599§	D7624§	D7649§	D7674§
D7522§	D7548§	D7574§	D7600§	D7625§	D7650§	D7675§
D7523§	D7549§	D7575§	D7601§	D7626§	D7651§	D7676§
D7524§	D7550§	D7576§	D7602§	D7627§	D7652§	D7677§
D7525§	D7551§	D7577§				

TOTAL: 477

Type I   English Electric   Bo-Bo

Introduced
1957

Total b.h.p.
1,000

★

Engine
English Electric 8 SVT Mk. II of 1,000 b.h.p. at 850 r.p.m. (continuous)

Transmission
Electric. Four axle-hung, nose-suspended d.c. traction motors

Weight
72 tons

Driving wheel diameter
3′ 7″

Maximum tractive effort
42,000 lb

D8000	D8029	D8058	D8087	D8116	D8144	D8172
D8001	D8030	D8059	D8088	D8117	D8145	D8173
D8002	D8031	D8060	D8089	D8118	D8146	D8174
D8003	D8032	D8061	D8090	D8119	D8147	D8175
D8004	D8033	D8062	D8091	D8120	D8148	D8176
D8005	D8034	D8063	D8092	D8121	D8149	D8177
D8006	D8035	D8064	D8093	D8122	D8150	D8178
D8007	D8036	D8065	D8094	D8123	D3151	D8179
D8008	D8037	D8066	D8095	D8124	D8152	D8180
D8009	D8038	D8067	D8096	D8125	D8153	D8181
D8010	D8039	D8068	D8097	D8126	D8154	D8182
D8011	D8040	D8069	D8098	D8127	D8155	D8183
D8012	D8041	D8070	D8099	D8128	D8156	D8184
D8013	D8042	D8071	D8100	D8129	D8157	D8185
D8014	D8043	D8072	D8101	D8130	D8158	D8186
D8015	D8044	D8073	D8102	D8131	D8159	D8187
D8016	D8045	D8074	D8103	D8132	D8160	D8188
D8017	D8046	D8075	D8104	D8133	D8161	D8189
D8018	D8047	D8076	D8105	D8134	D8162	D8190
D8019	D8048	D8077	D8106	D8135	D8163	D8191
D8020	D8049	D8078	D8107	D8136	D8164	D8192
D8021	D8050	D8079	D8108	D8137	D8165	D8193
D8022	D8051	D8080	D8109	D8138	D8166	D8194
D8023	D8052	D8081	D8110	D8139	D8167	D8195
D8024	D8053	D8082	D8111	D8140	D8168	D8196
D8025	D8054	D8083	D8112	D8141	D8169	D8197
D8026	D8055	D8084	D8113	D8142	D8170	D8198
D8027	D8056	D8085	D8114	D8143	D8171	D8199
D8028	D8057	D8086	D8115			

Class continued with D8300

English Electric Type 1 1,000 b.h.p. diesel-electric Bo-Bo No. D8101   [*D. L. Percival*

English Electric Type 1 1,000 b.h.p. diesel-electric Bo-Bo Nos. D8163 and D8191 (in blue livery)   [*D. L. Percival*

British Thomson-Houston Type 1 800 b.h.p. diesel-electric Bo-Bo No. D8238   [*D. L. Percival*

Type 1   British Thomson-Houston   Bo-Bo

Introduced
1957

Engine
Paxman 16-cyl YHXL V-type, pressure charged, of 800 b.h.p. at 1,250 r.p.m.

Weight
68 tons

Maximum tractive effort
37,500 lb

Total b.h.p.
800   ★

Transmission
Electric Four B.T.H. nose-suspended traction motors with single reduction gear drive

Driving wheel diameter
3′ 3½″

D8200	D8207	D8214	D8220	D8226	D8232	D8238
D8201	D8208	D8215	D8221	D8227	D8233	D8239
D8202	D8209	D8216	D8222	D8228	D8234	D8240
D8203	D8210	D8217	D8223	D8229	D8235	D8241
D8204	D8211	D8218	D8224	D8230	D8236	D8242
D8205	D8212	D8219	D8225	D8231	D8237	D8243
D8206	D8213					

TOTAL: 44

Type 1   English Electric   Bo-Bo

Class continued from D8199   ✴

D8300	D8304	D8308	D8312	D8316	D8320	D8324
D8301	D8305	D8309	D8313	D8317	D8321	D8325
D8302	D8306	D8310	D8314	D8318	D8322	D8326
D8303	D8307	D8311	D8315	D8319	D8323	D8327

TOTAL: 228

Type 1   North British   Bo-Bo

Introduced
1958

Engine
Paxman 16-cyl 16YHXL of 800 b.h.p. at 1,250 r.p.m.

Weight
68 tons

Maximum tractive effort
42,000 lb

Total b.h.p.
800   ●

Transmission
Electric. Four G.E.C. axle-hung nose-suspended traction motors

Driving wheel diameter
3′ 7″

D8400	D8402	D8404	D8406	D8407	D8408	D8409
D840	D8403	D8405				

TOTAL: 10

Type 1   Clayton   Bo-Bo

Introduced
1962

Engines
Two Paxman 6-cyl 6ZHXL of 450 b.h.p. at 1,500 r.p.m.
*Two Rolls-Royce 8-cyl. Type D of 450 b.h.p.

Weight
68 tons

Maximum tractive effort
40,000 lb

Total b.h.p.
900   ◆ ★ †

Transmission
Electric. Four G.E.C. axle-hung nose-suspended traction motors
†Four Crompton Parkinson traction motors.

Driving wheel diameter
3′ 3½″

North British Type 800 b.h.p. diesel electric Bo-Bo No. D8403
[D. L. Percival]

Clayton Type 1 900 b.h.p. diesel-electric Bo-Bo No. D8587 (with Rolls-Royce engines)
[D. L. Percival]

Clayton Type 1 900 b.h.p. diesel-electric Bo-Bo No. D8593
[D. L. Percival]

D8500	D8517	D8534	D8551	D8568	D8585	D8601†
D8501	D8518	D8535	D8552	D8569	D8586*	D8602†
D8502	D8519	D8536	D8553	D8570	D8587*	D8603†
D8503	D8520	D8537	D8554	D8571	D8588†	D8604†
D8504	D8521	D8538	D8555	D8572	D8589†	D8605†
D8505	D8522	D8539	D8556	D8573	D8590†	D8606†
D8506	D8523	D8540	D8557	D8574	D8591†	D8607†
D8507	D8524	D8541	D8558	D8575	D8592†	D8608†
D8508	D8525	D8542	D8559	D8576	D8593†	D8609†
D8509	D8526	D8543	D8560	D8577	D8594†	D8610†
D8510	D8527	D8544	D8561	D8578	D8595†	D8611†
D8511	D8528	D8545	D8562	D8579	D8596†	D8612†
D8512	D8529	D8546	D8563	D8580	D8597†	D8613†
D8513	D8530	D8547	D8564	D8581	D8598†	D8614†
D8514	D8531	D8548	D8565	D8582	D8599†	D8615†
D8515	D8532	D8549	D8566	D8583	D8600†	D8616†
D8516	D8533	D8550	D8567	D8584		

TOTAL: 117

Type 5   English-Electric   Co-Co

"Deltic"

Introduced
1961

Engines
Two 18-cyl Napier "Deltic" 18-25 of 1,650 b.h.p. at 1,500 r.p.m.

Weight
99 tons

Maximum tractive effort
50,000 lb

Total b.h.p.
3,300

Transmission
Electric. Six English Electric EE750 25G axle-hung nose-suspended traction motors

Driving wheel diameter
3′ 7″

* Fitted with train air brake equipment

D9000* Royal Scots Grey
D9001 St. Paddy
D9002 The King's Own Yorkshire Light Infantry
D9003 Meld
D9004 Queen's Own Highlander
D9005 The Prince of Wales's Own Regiment of Yorkshire
D9006 The Fife and Forfar Yeomanry
D9007* Pinza
D9008 The Green Howards
D9009 Alycidon
D9010 The King's Own Scottish Borderer
D9011 The Royal Northumberland Fusiliers
D9012 Crepello
D9013* The Black Watch
D9014 The Duke of Wellington's Regiment
D9015 Tulyar
D9016* Gordon Highlander
D9017 The Durham Light Infantry
D9018 Ballymoss
D9019* Royal Highland Fusilier
D9020* Nimbus
D9021* Argyll and Sutherland Highlander

TOTAL: 22

English Electric Type 5 3,300 b.h.p. diesel-electric Co-Co No. D9020 *Nimbus* (in blue livery) [*D. L. Percival*]

British Railways Type I 650 b.h.p. diesel-hydraulic 0-6-0 No. D9500. [*C. Firminger/OTA*

LMS 350 b.h.p. diesel-electric 0-6-0 No. 12009 (since withdrawn) [*J. E. Wilkinson*

Type 1   British Railways   0-6-0

Introduced
1964

Engine
Paxman 6-cyl "Ventura" 6YJX of 650
b.h.p. at 1,500 r.p.m.

Weight
50 tons

Maximum tractive effort
30,910 lb

Total b.h.p.
650

Transmission
Hydraulic. Voith L217U

Driving wheel diameter
4' 0"

D9500	D9508	D9516	D9524	D9532	D9540	D9548
D9501	D9509	D9517	D9525	D9533	D9541	D9549
D9502	D9510	D9518	D9526	D9534	D9542	D9550
D9503	D9511	D9519	D9527	D9535	D9543	D9551
D9504	D9512	D9520	D9528	D9536	D9544	D9552
D9505	D9513	D9521	D9529	D9537	D9545	D9553
D9506	D9514	D9522	D9530	D9538	D9546	D9554
D9507	D9515	D9523	D9531	D9539	D9547	D9555

TOTAL: 56

Shunter   L.M.S.   0-6-0

Introduced
1939

Engine
English Electric 6-cyl of 350 b.h.p.

Weight
54 tons 16 cwt

Maximum tractive effort
33,000 lb

Total b.h.p.
350

Transmission
Electric. Single motor, jackshaft
drive

Driving wheel diameter
4' 3"

12004	12012	12023	12024	12031	12032

TOTAL: 6

Shunter		L.M.S. and				0-6-0
		British Railways				

Introduced
1945

Engine
English Electric 6-cyl of 350 b.h.p.

Weight
47 tons 5 cwt

Maximum tractive effort
35,000 lb

Total b.h.p.
350

Transmission
Electric. Two nose-suspended motors, double reduction gear drive

Driving wheel diameter
4' 0½"

12033	12048	12063	12078	12093	12109	12124
12034	12049	12064	12079	12094	12110	12125
12035	12050	12065	12080	12095	12111	12126
12036	12051	12066	12081	12096	12112	12127
12037	12052	12067	12082	12097	12113	12128
12038	12053	12068	12083	12098	12114	12130
12039S	12054	12069	12084	12099	12115	12131
12040	12055	12070	12085	12100	12116	12132
12041	12056	12071	12086	12101	12117	12133
12042	12057	12072	12087	12102	12118	12134
12043	12058	12073	12088	12103	12119	12135
12044	12059	12074	12089	12105	12120	12136
12045	12060	12075	12090	12106	12121	12137
12046	12061	12076	12091	12107	12122	12138
12047S	12062S	12077	12092	12108		

TOTAL: 103

Shunter		British Railways				0-6-0

Introduced
1949

Engine
English Electric 6-cyl of 350 b.h.p.

Weight
45 tons

Maximum tractive effort
24,000 lb

Total b.h.p.
350

Transmission
Electric. Two nose-suspended motors, double reduction gear drive

Driving wheel diameter
4' 6"

15211	15215	15219	15223	15227	15231	15234
15212	15216	15220	15224	15228	15232	15235
15213	15217	15221	15225	15229	15233	15236
15214	15218	15222	15226	15230		

TOTAL: 26

Right: LMS 350 b.h.p. diesel-electric 0-6-0 No. 12090
[D. L. Percival

Centre: British Railways 350 b.h.p. diesel-electric 0-6-0 No. 15212 (in blue livery)
[D. L. Percival

Bottom: Brush Type 4 2,700 b.h.p. diesel-electric Co-Co No. D0280 Falcon
[D. L. Percival

LOCOMOTIVES ON TRIAL

British Railways are providing facilities for road tests of the following locomotives, which remain the property of the manufacturers and are not included in B.R. stock.

Type 4   Brush   Co-Co

Introduced
1961

Engines
Two Maybach MD655 V-type of 1,440 b.h.p. at 1500 r.p.m.

Weight
115 tons

Maximum tractive effort
60,000 lb

D0280 *Falcon*

Total b.h.p.
2,700

Transmission
Electric. Six Brush traction motors

Driving wheel diameter
3' 7"

Type 4   English Electric   Co-Co

Introduced
1962

Engine
English Electric 16-cyl. 16CSVT, after-cooled, of 2,700 b.h.p.

Weight
105 tons

Maximum tractive effort
50,000 lb

DP2

Total b.h.p.
2,700

Transmission
Electric

Driving wheel diameter
3' 6"

Brush   Co-Co

Introduced
1968

Engines
Sulzer 16-cyl. 16LVA24, of 3,946 h.p. at 1,100 r.p.m.

Weight
126 tons

Maximum tractive effort
70,000 lb

HS4000 *Kestrel*

Total b.h.p.
4,000

Transmission
Electric. Six Brush 515 h.p. nose-suspended traction motors

Driving wheel diameter
3' 9"

DEPARTMENTAL LOCOMOTIVES

EASTERN & NORTH EASTERN REGIONS

Shunter   Hibberd & Co.   0-4-0

Introduced
1950

Engine
English National 4-cyl Gas type DA4
of 52 b.h.p. at 1,250 r.p.m.

Weight
11 tons

Maximum tractive effort

Total b.h.p.
52

Transmission
Mechanical. Spur-type three-speed
gearbox with roller chains

Driving wheel diameter

(Original number in brackets)

52 (11104)

Shunter   Ruston & Hornsby   0-4-0

Introduced
1955

Engine
Ruston & Hornsby Mark 4V vertical
4-cyl of 88 b.h.p.

Weight
17 tons

Maximum tractive effort
9,500 lb

56

Total b.h.p.
88

Transmission
Mechanical

Driving wheel diameter
3' 0"

Shunter   Barclay   0-4-0

Introduced
1958

Engine

Weight

Maximum tractive effort

Total b.h.p.
150

Transmission
Mechanical

Driving wheel diameter

82   83

Shunter   Ruston & Hornsby   0-4-0

Introduced
1959

Engine

Weight

Maximum tractive effort

Total b.h.p.
88

Transmission
Mechanical

Driving wheel diameter

84   85   87

Shunter   Hunslet   0-6-0

Introduced
1955

Engine
Gardner 8L3 of 204 b.h.p. at 1,200 r.p.m.

Weight
30 tons

Maximum tractive effort
14,500 lb

Total b.h.p.
204

Transmission
Mechanical. Hunslet patent friction clutch. Hunslet four-speed gearbox incorporating reverse and final drive gears

Driving wheel diameter
3′ 9″

(Original number in brackets)

88 (D2612)   89 (D2615)

LONDON MIDLAND REGION

Shunter   John Fowler & Co.   0-4-0

Introduced
1936

Engine
Fowler 4C vertical of 150 b.h.p. at 1,000 r.p.m. (1 hr rating)

Weight
29 tons

Maximum tractive effort
15,000 lb

Total b.h.p.
150

Transmission
Mechanical. Four-speed gearbox

Driving wheel diameter
3′ 3″

ED3   ED6

Fowler 150 b.h.p. diesel-mechanical 0-4-0 No. ED3

Ruston & Hornsby 165 b.h.p. diesel-electric 0-6-0 No. PWM651   [*D. L. Percival*]

SOUTHERN REGION

Shunter   Ruston & Hornsby   0-4-0

Introduced
1946

Engine
Ruston 4VRH

Weight
7 tons 10 cwt

Maximum tractive effort
3,480 lb

Total b.h.p.
48

Transmission
Mechanical. Chain drive

Driving wheel diameter
2' 6"

This locomotive was supplied to the Bristol Aviation Co. in 1946 and was later purchased by British Railways

DS1169

WESTERN REGION

Shunter   Ruston & Hornsby   0-4-0

Introduced
1957

Engine
Ruston & Hornsby 4-cyl of 88 b.h.p.

Weight
17 tons

Maximum tractive effort
9,500 lb

Total b.h.p.
88

Transmission
Mechanical. Chain driven from gearbox

Driving wheel diameter
3' 0"

20

Shunter   Ruston & Hornsby   0-6-0

Introduced
1953

Engine
Ruston & Hornsby 6-cyl of 165 b.h.p.

Weight
30 tons

Maximum tractive effort
17,000 lb

Total b.h.p.
165

Transmission
Electric. One B.T.H. nose-suspended traction motor

Driving wheel diameter
3' 2½"

PWM650   PWM651   PWM652   PWM653   PWM654

EASTERN REGION DIESEL
LOCOMOTIVE CLASSIFICATION

Horse-power	Description	Locomotive Nos.	Code
153	Hunslet/Gardner	D2950–2	1/15
153	Barclay/Gardner	D2953–6	1/12
165	Ruston & Hornsby ...	D2957–8	1/16
170	Yorkshire Engine Co.	D2850–69	1/17
200	N.B. Loco. Co./Paxman	D2700–7	2/4A
204	B.R./Gardner	D2000–2199, 2372–99 ...	2/1
204	Drewry/Gardner (3' 3" wheel) ...	D2200–14 ...	2/13A
204	Drewry/Gardner (3' 6" wheel) ...	D2215–73 ...	2/13
204	Drewry/Gardner (3' 7" wheel) ...	D2274–2340 ...	2/13
204	Barclay/Gardner (4-speed) ...	D2400–9	2/12A
204	Barclay/Gardner (5-speed) ...	D2410–44	2/12
204	Hudswell-Clarke/Gardner ...	D2500–19 ...	2/14
204	Hunslet/Gardner (3' 4" wheel) ...	D2550–73	2/15A
204	Hunslet/Gardner (3' 9" wheel) ...	D2574–D2618 ...	2/15
225	N.B. Loco. Co./M.A.N.	D2708–80	2/4
275	Ruston/Paxman	D2985–98	2/16
350	B.R./English Electric	D3000–3116/27–36/67 –3438/54–72, 3503– 3611/52–64/72–96/9– 371,8/22–4048/95– 4186/91/2 ...	3/1
350	B.R./Blackstone/G.E.C.	D3137–51, 3439–53/ 73–3502, 3612–51 4049–94 ...	3/1C
350	B.R./E.E. (max. speed 27 m.p.h.)	D3665–71, 3719–21 ...	3/1A
350	L.M.S./English Electric (4' 3" wheel)	12003–32	3/8
350	L.M.S./English Electric (4' 0½" wheel)	12033–12138 ...	3/8A
350	S.R./English Electric	15211–36	3/9
700	B.R./English Electric	D4500–2	7/1
800	B.T.H./Paxman	D8200–43	8/5
800	N.B. Loco. Co./Paxman	D8400–9	8/4
900	Clayton/Paxman	D8500–8616 ...	9/18
1,000	N.B. Loco. Co./M.A.N./G.E.C. ...	D6100–6137 ...	10/4
1,000	N.B. Loco. Co./M.A.N./Voith ...	D6300–5	10/4A
1,000	English Electric	D8000–8199, 8300–27 ...	10/3
1,100	English Electric/Napier	D5900–9	11/3
1,100	N.B. Loco. Co./M.A.N./G.E.C. ...	D6138–57	11/4
1,100	N.B. Loco. Co./M.A.N./Voith ...	D6306–57	11/4A
1,160	B.R./Sulzer	D5000–49	11/1
1,160	B.R./Sulzer	D5050–5150 ...	11/1A
1,160	Birmingham/Sulzer	D5300–46	11/6
1,200	Metro. Vickers/Crossley	D5700–19	12/5
1,250	Brush/Mirrlees	D5500–5699, 5800– 34/6–62 ...	12/2*
1,250	Birmingham/Sulzer	D5347–5415 ...	12/6

1,250	B.R./Sulzer	D5151–5299 ...	12/1
1,550	Birmingham/Sulzer	D6500–85	15/6
1,550	Birmingham/Sulzer	D6586–97	15/6A
1,600	Brush/Mirrlees	D5835	16/2
1,700	Beyer Peacock/Maybach	D7000–7100 ...	17/7
1,750	English Electric	D6600–8, 6700–6958, 6969–99	17/3
1,750	English Electric (air-braked) ...	D6959–68	17/3A
2,000	B.R./Maybach/Mekydro	D800–2	20/1
2,000	English Electric	D200–399	20/3
2,000	N.B. Loco. Co./M.A.N./Voith ...	D600–4	20/4
2,200	B.R./Maybach/Mekydro	D803–29/31/2/66–70	22/1
2,200	N.B. Loco. Co.	D833–65	22/4
2,300	B.R./Sulzer	D1–10 ...	23/1
2,500	B.R./Sulzer	D11–137	25/1
2,500	B.R./Sulzer/Brush	D138–93	25/1A
2,650	Brush/Sulzer	D1702–6	26/2
2,700	B.R./Maybach/Voith	D1000–73	27/1
2,750	Brush/Sulzer	D1500–1630/82–1701/7–57	27/2
2,750	Brush/Sulzer (air-braked) ...	D1100–11, 1631–81, 1758–1999	27/2A
3,300	English Electric/Napier Deltic ...	D9000–21	33/3 †

* 1,470 b.h.p. locomotives are classified 14/2

† Air-braked locomotives are classified 33/3A

B.R. DIESEL MULTIPLE-UNITS

UNLESS otherwise stated, all multiple-unit trains are gangwayed within each set, with guard's and luggage compartment at the inner end of motor brake coaches, and seating is in open saloons with centre and/or end doors. The letter (L) in the headings indicates an open vehicle fitted with toilet facilities; (K) indicates a side corridor vehicle with toilet. Two standard lengths of underframe are in use, namely 56ft 11in and 63ft 5in, but the actual body lengths vary by a few inches for the same type of underframe. The dimensions shown are the length over body and the overall width.

Several of the types listed are sub-divided by reason of detail or mechanical differences. For example, a certain number of cars in a class may have different seating arrangement or a different make of engine but are otherwise similar to the main batch. Such differences are noted in the heading to the class and given a reference mark by which the relevant dimensions or details and the cars concerned can be identified. The type of set in which each class is formed on delivery, together with the principal manufacturer, is shown at the head of the details for that class, although it should be noted that changes may occur owing to varying operating conditions, even to the extent of coupling different makes of car in the same set or running power cars without intermediate trailers. Most railcars are fitted with a standard Mechanical transmission of a cardan shaft and freewheel to a four-speed epicyclic gearbox, and a further cardan shaft to the final drive. Where a non-standard transmission is employed, full details are shown under the relevant heading. Cars are listed in numerical order by type and not by set formation.

COUPLING CODES

Although several multiple-unit diesel sets can be coupled together and driven by one man in the leading cab, for various reasons it is not possible for all types of diesel unit to work together. In order to distinguish cars that can run together, all have painted at each end above the buffers a colour code symbol. A miniature symbol also appears on the plug socket covers. Only units bearing the same symbol may be coupled together.

★ ORANGE STAR   ● WHITE CIRCLE

◆ YELLOW DIAMOND   ■ BLUE SQUARE

Derby 3-car suburban unit with motor brake second No. W50060 leading at Hall Green
[M. Mensing

Metro-Cammell motor brake second No. NE50286 [D. L. Percival

Birmingham R.C. & W. Co. motor brake second No. M50538 [P. J. Sharpe

NUMERICAL LIST OF
DIESEL MULTIPLE-UNITS

Derby Works, B.R. (2)
MOTOR BRAKE SECOND ◼

Introduced: 1956

Engines
Two B.U.T. (Leyland) 6-cyl. horizontal type of 230 b.h.p.
* Two B.U.T. (Leyland) 6-cyl. horizontal type of 230 b.h.p.
Body: 64′ 6″ × 9′ 3″
Seats: 2nd, 62

Transmission
Mechanical. Standard
* Mechanical. Standard. Fitted with Self Changing Gears Ltd. automatic four-speed gearbox
Weight: 35 tons 10 cwt (37 tons 10 cwt*)

E50001	E50009	E50017	E50025	E50034	E50042
E50002	E50010	E50018	E50026	E50035	E50043
E50003	E50011	E50019	E50027	E50036	E50044
E50004	E50012	E50020	E50029	E50037	E50045
E50005	E50013	E50021	E50030	E50038	E50046
E50006	E50014	E50022	E50031	E50039	E50047
E50007	E50015	E50023	E50032	E50040	E50048
E50008	E50016	E50024	E50033	E50041	E50049 *

Derby Works, B.R. (3 Suburban)
MOTOR BRAKE SECOND ◼

Introduced: 1957

Engines
Two B.U.T. (Leyland) 6-cyl. horizontal type of 150 b.h.p.

Transmission
Mechanical. Standard

Body: 64′ 0″ × 9′ 3″. Non-gangwayed, side doors to each seating bay
Weight: 35 tons 10 cwt   **Seats: 2nd,** 65

M50050	M50057	M50064	M50071	M 50078	M 50085
M50051	M50058	M50065	M50072	M 50079	W50086
M50052	M50059	M50066	M50073	W50080	W50087
M50053	M50060	M50067	M50074	W50081	W50088
M50054	M50061	M50068	M50075	W50082	W50089
M50055	M50062	M50069	M50076	W50083	W50090
M50056	M50063	M50070	M50077	W50084	W50091

Derby Works, B.R. (3 Suburban)
MOTOR SECOND ◼

Introduced: 1957

Engines
Two B.U.T. (Leyland) 6-cyl. horizontal type of 150 b.h.p.

Transmission
Mechanical. Standard

Body: 64′ 0″ × 9′ 3″. Non-gangwayed, side doors to each seating bay
Weight: 35 tons 10 cwt   **Seats: 2nd,** 95

M50092	M50099	M50106	M50113	M 50120	W50128
M50093	M50100	M50107	M50114	M 50121	W50129
M50094	M50101	M50108	M50115	W50122	W50130
M50095	M50102	M50109	M50116	W50123	W50131
	M50103	M50110	M50117	W50124	W50132
M50097	M50104	M50111	M50118	W50126	W50133
M50098	M50105	M50112	M50119	M 50127	

Metropolitan-Cammell (2)
MOTOR BRAKE SECOND ■

Introduced: 1957

Engines
Two Rolls-Royce 6-cyl. horizontal
type of 180 b.h.p.

Transmission
Mechanical. Standard

Body: 57' 0" × 9' 3" **Weight:** 33 tons **Seats: 2nd, 52**

NE50134   NE50135   NE50136   NE50137

Metropolitan-Cammell (4)
MOTOR COMPOSITE (L) ■

Introduced: 1956

Engines
Two B.U.T. (A.E.C.) 6-cyl. horizontal
type of 150 b.h.p.

Transmission
Mechanical. Standard

Body: 57' 0" × 9' 3" **Weight:** 32 tons **Seats: 1st, 12; 2nd, 45**

NE50138	NE50141	NE50144	NE50146	NE50148	NE50150
NE50139	NE50142	NE50145	NE50147	NE50149	NE50151
NE50140	NE50143				

Metropolitan-Cammell (2)
MOTOR BRAKE SECOND ■

Introduced: 1956

Engines
Two B.U.T. (A.E.C.) 6-cyl. horizontal
type of 150 b.h.p.

Transmission
Mechanical. Standard

Body: 57' 0" × 9' 3" **Weight:** 32 tons **Seats: 2nd, 52**

E50152   E50153   NE50154   NE50155   NE50156   NE50157

Metropolitan-Cammell (2)
MOTOR COMPOSITE (L) ■

Introduced: 1956

Engines
Two B.U.T. (A.E.C.) 6-cyl. horizontal
type of 150 b.h.p.

Transmission
Mechanical. Standard

Body: 57' 0" × 9' 3" **Weight:** 32 tons **Seats: 1st, 12; 2nd, 53**

E50158   E50159   NE50160   NE50161   NE50162   NE50163

Metropolitan-Cammell (2)

MOTOR BRAKE SECOND ■

Introduced: 1957

For details see E50152-NE50157

NE50164 NE50165 NE50166 NE50167

Metropolitan-Cammell (2)

MOTOR COMPOSITE (L) ■

Introduced: 1957

For details see E50158-NE50163

NE50168 NE50169 NE50170 NE50171

Metropolitan-Cammell (4)

MOTOR COMPOSITE (L) ■

Introduced: 1957

For details see E50158-NE50163

NE50172	NE50178	NE50182	E50186	NE50190	NE50194
E50174	NE50179	NE50183	E50187	NE50191	NE50195
E50175	NE50180	NE50184	NE50188	NE50192	NE50196
NE50176	NE50181	NE50185	NE50189	NE50193	NE50197
NE50177					

Metropolitan-Cammell (2)

MOTOR BRAKE SECOND ■

Introduced: 1957

For details see E50152-NE50157

NE50198	NE50204	NE50210	NE50216	NE50222	M50228
NE50199	NE50205	NE50211	NE50217	NE50223	NE50229
NE50200	M50206	NE50212	NE50218	NE50224	NE50230
NE50201	NE50207	NE50213	NE50219	NE50225	NE50231
NE50202	M50208	NE50214	NE50220	NE50226	NE50232
M50203	NE50209	NE50215	NE50221	NE50227	NE50233

Metropolitan-Cammell (4)

MOTOR COMPOSITE (L) ■

Introduced: 1957

For details see NE50138-51

NE50234	NE50237	NE50239	NE50241	NE50243	NE50245
NE50235	NE50238	NE50240	NE50242	NE50244	

Metropolitan-Cammell (2)
MOTOR BRAKE SECOND ■
Introduced: 1957

Engines
Two B.U.T. (A.E.C.) 6-cyl. horizontal type of 150 b.h.p.

Transmission
Mechanical. Standard

Body: 57′ 0″ × 9′ 3″   **Weight:** 32 tons   **Seats:** 2nd, 44

NE50246   NE50247   NE50248

Cravens (4)
MOTOR BRAKE SECOND ■
Introduced: 1959

Engines
Two B.U.T. (A.E.C.) 6-cyl. horizontal type of 150 b.h.p.

Transmission
Mechanical. Standard

Body: 57′ 6″ × 9′ 2″   **Weight:** 30 tons 10 cwt   **Seats:** 2nd, 52

NE50249

Metropolitan-Cammell (2)
MOTOR BRAKE SECOND ■
Introduced: 1957

Engines
Two B.U.T. (A.E.C.) 6-cyl. horizontal type of 150 b.h.p.

Transmission
Mechanical. Standard

Body: 57′ 0″ × 9′ 3″   **Weight:** 32 tons   **Seats:** 2nd, 52

NE50250   NE50252   NE50254   NE50256   NE50258   NE50259
NE50251   NE50253   NE50255   NE50257

Metropolitan-Cammell (2)
MOTOR COMPOSITE (L) ■
Introduced: 1957

Engines
Two B.U.T. (A.E.C.) 6-cyl. horizontal type of 150 b.h.p.

Transmission
Mechanical. Standard

Body: 57′ 0″ × 9′ 3″   **Weight:** 32 tons   **Seats:** 1st, 12; 2nd, 53

NE50260   NE50262   NE50264   NE50266   NE50268   NE50269
NE50261   NE50263   NE50265   NE50267

Metropolitan-Cammell (3)
MOTOR COMPOSITE (L) ■
Introduced: 1957

Engines
Two Rolls-Royce 6-cyl. horizontal type of 180 b.h.p.

Transmission
Mechanical. Standard

Body: 57′ 0″ × 9′ 3″   **Weight:** 33 tons   **Seats:** 1st, 12; 2nd, 53

NE50270   NE50272   NE50274   NE50276   NE50278   NE50279
NE50271   NE50273   NE50275   NE50277

Metropolitan-Cammell (3)
MOTOR BRAKE SECOND
Introduced: 1957

Engines
Two Rolls-Royce 6-cyl. horizontal
type of 180 b.h.p.

Transmission
Mechanical. Standard

Body: 57′ 0″ × 9′ 3″   **Weight:** 33 tons   **Seats: 2nd,** 52

NE50280	NE50282	NE50284	NE50287	NE50289	E50291
NE50281	NE50283	NE50286	NE50288	E50290	E50292

Metropolitan-Cammell (2)
MOTOR BRAKE SECOND
Introduced: 1957

Engines
Two B.U.T. (A.E.C.) 6-cyl. horizontal
type of 150 b.h.p.

Transmission
Mechanical. Standard

Body: 57′ 0″ × 9′ 3″   **Weight:** 32 tons   **Seats: 2nd,** 52

NE50293	NE50294	NE50295	NE50296

Metropolitan-Cammell (3)
MOTOR BRAKE SECOND
Introduced: 1958

Engines
Two B.U.T. (A.E.C.) 6-cyl. horizontal
type of 150 b.h.p.

Transmission
Mechanical. Standard

Body: 57′ 0″ × 9′ 3″   **Weight:** 31 tons 10 cwt   **Seats: 2nd,** 52

M50303	M50306	M50309	M50312	M50315	M50318
M50304	M50307	M50310	M50313	M50316	M50319
M50305	M50308	M50311	M50314	M50317	M50320

Metropolitan-Cammell (3)
MOTOR COMPOSITE (L)
Introduced: 1958

Engines
Two B.U.T. (A.E.C.) 6-cyl. horizontal
type of 150 b.h.p.

Transmission
Mechanical. Standard

Body: 57′ 0″ × 9′ 3″   **Weight:** 32 tons   **Seats: 1st,** 12; **2nd,** 53

M50321	M50324	M50327	M50330	M50333	M50336
M50322	M50325	M50328	M50331	M50334	M50337
M50323	M50326	M50329	M50332	M50335	M50338

Gloucester R.C. & W. Co. (2)
MOTOR BRAKE SECOND
Introduced: 1957

Engines
Two B.U.T. (A.E.C.) 6-cyl. horizontal
type of 150 b.h.p.

Transmission
Mechanical. Standard
* Fitted with C.A.V. Ltd. automatic
gear change equipment

Body: 57′ 6″ × 9′ 3″   **Weight:** 30 tons 5 cwt   **Seats: 2nd,** 52

SC50339	SC50343	SC50347	M50350	M50353	M50356
SC50340	SC50344	M50348	M50351	M50354	M50357
SC50341	SC50345	M50349	M50352	M50355	M50358*
SC50342	SC50346				

Cravens (2)
MOTOR BRAKE SECOND ■

Introduced: 1956

Engines
Two B.U.T. (Leyland) (A.E.C.*) 6-cyl.
horizontal type of 150 b.h.p

Transmission
Mechanical. Standard

Body: 57′ 6″ × 9′ 2″   **Weight:** 29 tons   **Seats: 2nd, 52**

NE50359	NE50365	NE50371*	E50377*	E50383*	NE50389*
E50360	E50366	NE50372*	NE50378*	E50384*	M50390*
NE50361	NE50367	NE50373*	NE50379*	NE50385*	M50391*
E50362	NE50368	NE50374*	NE50380*	NE50386*	M50392*
NE50363	NE50369	NE50375*	NE50381*	NE50387*	M50393*
NE50364	NE50370	E50376*	NE50382*	NE50388*	M50394*

Park Royal Vehicles (2)
MOTOR BRAKE SECOND ■

Introduced: 1957

Engines
Two B.U.T. (A.E.C.) 6-cyl. horizontal
type of 150 b.h.p.

Transmission
Mechanical. Standard

Body: 57′ 6″ × 9′ 3″   **Weight:** 33 tons 8 cwt   **Seats: 2nd, 52**

M50395	M50399	M50403	M50406	M50409	M50412
M50396	M50400	M50404	M50407	M50410	M50413
M50397	M50401	M50405	M50408	M50411	M50414
M50398	M50402				

D. Wickham & Co. (2)
MOTOR BRAKE SECOND ■

Introduced: 1957

Engines
Two B.U.T. (Leyland) 6-cyl. horizontal type of 150 b.h.p.

Transmission
Mechanical. Standard

Body: 57′ 0″ × 9′ 3″   **Weight:** 27 tons 10 cwt   **Seats: 2nd, 59**

E50417	E50418

Birmingham R. C. & W. Co. (3)
MOTOR BRAKE SECOND ■

Introduced: 1957

Engines
Two B.U.T. (Leyland) 6-cyl. horizontal type of 150 b.h.p.

Transmission
Mechanical. Standard

Body: 57′ 6″ × 9′ 3″   **Weight:** 31 tons   **Seats: 2nd, 52**

M50420	M50421	M50422	M50423

Birmingham R. C. & W. Co. (3)
MOTOR COMPOSITE (L) ■

Introduced: 1957

Engines
Two B.U.T. (Leyland) 6-cyl. horizontal type of 150 b.h.p.

Transmission
Mechanical. Standard

Body: 57′ 6″ × 9′ 3″   **Weight:** 31 tons   **Seats:** 1st, 12; 2nd, 54

M50424	M50425	M50426	M50427

Birmingham R. C. & W. Co. (3)
MOTOR BRAKE SECOND ■

Introduced: 1957

For details see M50420-3

M50428	M50437	M50446	M50455	M50464	M50472
M50429	M50438	M50447	M50456	M50465	M50473
M50430	M50439	M50448	M50457	M50466	M50474
M50431	M50440	M50449	M50458	M50467	M50475
M50432	M50441	M50450	M50459	M50468	M50476
M50433	M50442	M50451	M50460	M50469	M50477
M50434	M50443	M50452	M50461	M50470	M50478
M50435	M50444	M50453	M50462	M50471	M50479
M50436	M50445	M50454	M50463		

Birmingham R. C. & W. Co. (3)
MOTOR COMPOSITE (L) ■

Introduced: 1957

For details see M50424-7

M50480	M50489	M50498	M50507	M50516	M50524
M50481	M50490	M50499	M50508	M50517	M50525
M50482	M50491	M50500	M50509	M50518	M50526
M50483	M50492	M50501	M50510	M50519	M50527
M50484	M50493	M50502	M50511	M50520	M50528
M50485	M50494	M50503	M50512	M50521	M50529
M50486	M50495	M50504	M50514	M50522	M50530
M50487	M50496	M50505	M50515	M50523	M50531
M50488	M50497	M50506			

Birmimgham R. C. & W. Co. (2)
MOTOR BRAKE SECOND ■

Introduced: 1958

Engines
Two B.U.T. (Leyland) 6-cyl. horizontal type of 150 b.h.p.

Transmission
Mechanical. Standard

Body: 57′ 6″ × 9′ 3″   **Weight:** 31 tons   **Seats:** 2nd, 52

M50532 M50534 M50536 M50538 M50540 M50541
M50533 M50535 M50537 M50539

Birmingham R. C. & W. Co. (4)
MOTOR COMPOSITE (L) ■
Introduced: 1958

Engines
Two B.U.T. (Leyland) 6-cyl. horizontal type of 150 b.h.p.

Transmission
Mechanical. Standard

Body: 57′ 6″ × 9′ 3″   Weight: 31 tons   Seats: 1st, 12; 2nd, 51

NE50542	NE50551	NE50560	NE50569	NE50578	NE50586
NE50543	NE50552	NE50561	NE50570	NE50579	NE50587
NE50544	NE50553	NE50562	NE50571	NE50580	NE50588
NE50545	NE50554	NE50563	NE50572	NE50581	NE50589
NE50546	NE50555	NE50564	NE50573	NE50582	NE50590
NE50547	NE50556	NE50565	NE50574	NE50583	NE50591
NE50548	NE50557	NE50566	NE50575	NE50584	
NE50549		NE50567	NE50576	NE50585	N E50593
NE50550	N E50559	NE50568	NE50577		

Birmingham R. C. & W. Co. (2)
MOTOR BRAKE SECOND ■
Introduced: 1958

Engines
Two B.U.T. (Leyland) 6-cyl. horizontal type of 160 b.h.p.

Transmission
Mechanical. Standard

Body: 57′ 6″ × 9′ 3″   Weight: 31 tons   Seats: 2nd, 52

NE50594   NE50595   NE50596   NE50597   NE50598

Derby Works, B.R. (2 or 3*)
MOTOR BRAKE SECOND ■
Introduced: 1958

Engines
Two B.U.T. (Leyland) 6-cyl. horizontal type of 150 b.h.p.

Transmission
Mechanical. Standard

Body: 57′ 6″ × 9′ 2″   Weight: 28 tons 10 cwt   Seats: 2nd, 52

NE50599	NE50605	E50610	NE50615	E50620*	M50625
NE50600	NE50606		NE50616	E50621*	M50626
NE50601	NE50607	NE50612	NE50617	E50622*	M50627
NE50602	NE50608	NE50613	NE50618	E50623*	M50628
NE50603	NE50609	N E50614	NE50619	E50624*	M50629
NE50604					

Derby Works, B.R. (3* or 4)

MOTOR COMPOSITE (L) ∎

Introduced: 1958

Engines
Two B.U.T. (Leyland) 6-cyl. horizontal type of 150 b.h.p.

Transmission
Mechanical. Standard

Body: 57′ 6″ × 9′ 2″   **Weight:** 28 tons   **Seats:** 1st, 12; 2nd, 50

NE50630	E50633	NE50636	NE50639	E50642*	E50645*
NE50631	NE50634	NE50637	NE50640	E50643*	E50646*
E50632	NE50635	NE50638	NE50641	E50644*	

Swindon Works, B.R. (3 Cross Country)

MOTOR SECOND (L) ∎

Introduced: 1957

Engines
Two B.U.T. (A.E.C.) 6-cyl. horizontal type of 150 b.h.p.

Transmission
Mechanical. Standard

Body: 64′ 6″ × 9′ 3″   **Weight:** 36 tons 10 cwt   **Seats:** 2nd, 68

W50647	W50656	W50664	W50672	W50680	W50688
W50648	W50657	W50665	W50673	W50681	W50689
W50649	W50658	W50666	W50674	W50682	W50690
W50650	W50659	W50667	W50675	W50683	W50691
W50651	W50660	W50668	W50676	W50684	W50692
W50652	W50661	W50669	W50677	W50685	W50693
W50653	W50662	W50670	W50678	W50686	W50694
W50654	W50663	W50671	W50679	W50687	W50695
W50655					

Swindon Works, B.R. (3 Cross Country)

MOTOR BRAKE COMPOSITE ∎

Introduced: 1957

Engines
Two B.U.T. (A.E.C.) 6-cyl. horizontal type of 150 b.h.p.

Transmission
Mechanical. Standard

Body: 64′ 6″ × 9′ 3″   **Weight:** 36 tons   **Seats:** 1st, 18; 2nd, 16

W50696	W50705	W50713	W50721	W50729	W50737
W50697	W50706	W50714	W50722	W50730	W50738
W50698	W50707	W50715	W50723	W50731	W50739
W50699	W50708	W50716	W50724	W50732	W50740
W50700	W50709	W50717	W50725	W50733	W50741
W50701	W50710	W50718	W50726	W50734	W50742
W50702	W50711	W50719	W50727	W50735	W50743
W50703	W50712	W50720	W50728	W50736	W50744
W50704					

Swindon motor brake composite No. W50704   [D. L. Percival]

Derby 3-car suburban unit with motor second No. W50917 leading and Pressed Steel motor brake second No. W55034 near Radyr   [D. L. Percival]

Derby twin units with motor brake second No. M50981 leading   [P. J. Sharp]

Metropolitan-Cammell (3)
MOTOR COMPOSITE (L) ■

Introduced: 1957

Engines
Two Rolls-Royce 6-cyl. horizontal type of 180 b.h.p.

Transmission
Mechanical. Standard

Body: 57′ 0″ × 9′ 3″   **Weight:** 32 tons   **Seats:** 1st, 12; 2nd, 53

E50745	E50746	E50747

Metropolitan-Cammell (4)
MOTOR COMPOSITE (L) ■

Introduced: 1957

Engines
Two B.U.T. (A.E.C.) 6-cyl. horizontal type of 150 b.h.p.

Transmission
Mechanical. Standard

Body: 57′ 0″ × 9′ 3″   **Weight:** 32 tons   **Seats:** 1st, 12; 2nd, 53

NE50748	NE50749	NE50750	NE50751

Cravens (3)
MOTOR BRAKE SECOND ■

Introduced: 1957

Engines
Two B.U.T. (A.E.C.) 6-cyl. horizontal type of 150 b.h.p.

Transmission
Mechanical. Standard

Body: 57′ 6″ × 9′ 2″   **Weight:** 30 tons   **Seats:** 2nd, 52

M50752	M50756	M50759	M50762	M50765	M50768
M50753	M50757	M50760	M50763	M50766	M50769
M50754	M50758	M50761	M50764	M50767	M50770
M50755					

Cravens (2)
MOTOR BRAKE SECOND ■

Introduced: 1957

Engines
Two B.U.T. (A.E.C.) 6-cyl. horizontal type of 150 b.h.p.

Transmission
Mechanical. Standard

Weight: 30 tons   **Seats:** 2nd, 52

M50771	M50774	M50776	M50778	M50780	M50782
M50772	M50775	M50777	M50779	M50781	M50784
M50773					

Cravens (3)
MOTOR COMPOSITE (L) ■

Introduced: 1957

Engines
Two B.U.T. (A.E.C.) 6-cyl. horizontal type of 150 b.h.p.

Transmission
Mechanical. Standard

Body: 57′ 6″ × 9′ 2″   **Weight:** 30 tons   **Seats:** 1st, 12; 2nd, 51

M50785	M50789	M50792	M50795	M50798	M50801
M50786	M50790	M50793	M50796	M50799	M50802
M50787	M50791	M50794	M50797	M50800	M50803
M50788					

Cravens (2)

MOTOR COMPOSITE (L) ■

Introduced: 1958

Engines
Two B.U.T. (A.E.C.) 6-cyl. horizontal
type of 150 b.h.p.

Transmission
Mechanical. Standard

Body: 57′ 6″ × 9′ 2″   **Weight:** 30 tons   **Seats:** 1st, 12; 2nd, 51

M50804	M50807	M50810	M50812	M50814	M50816
M50805	M50809	M50811	M50813	M50815	M50817
M50806					

Derby Works, B.R. (3 Suburban)

MOTOR BRAKE SECOND ■

Introduced: 1957

For details see **M50050-W50091**

W50818	W50827	W50836	W50845	W50854	W50863
W50819	W50828	W50837	W50846	W50855	W50864
W50820	W50829	W50838	W50847	W50856	W50865
W50821	W50830	W50839	W50848	W50857	W50866
W50822	M 50831	W50840	W50849	W50858	W50867
W50823	W50832	W50841	W50850	M 50859	W50868
W50824	M 50833	W50842	W50851	M 50860	W50869
W50825	W50834	W50843	W50852	M 50861	W50870
W50826	W50835	W50844	W50853	W50862	

Derby Works, B.R. (3 Suburban)

MOTOR SECOND ■

Introduced: 1957

For details see **M50092-W50133**

W50871	W50880	W50889	W50898	W50907	W50916
W50872	W50881	W50890	W50899	W50908	W50917
W50873	W50882	W50891	W50900	W50909	W50918
W50874	W50883	W50892	W50901	W50910	W50919
W50875	M 50884	W50893	W50902	W50911	W50920
W50876	W50885	W50894	W50903	M50912	W50921
W50877	M 50886	W50895	W50904	M 50913	W50922
W50878	W50887	W50896	W50905	M 50914	W50923
W50879	W50888	W50897	W50906	W50915	

Derby Works, B.R. (2)
MOTOR BRAKE SECOND ■

Introduced: 1959

Engines
Two B.U.T. (Leyland) 6-cyl. horizontal type of 150 b.h.p.

Transmission
Mechanical. Standard

Body: 57′ 6″ × 9′ 2″ **Weight:** 28 tons 10 cwt **Seats:** 2nd, 52

M50924	M50926	M50928	M50930	M50932	M50934
M50925	M50927	M50929	M50931	M50933	M50935

Swindon Works, B.R. (6 Inter-City)
MOTOR SECOND (L) ●

Introduced: 1959

Engines
Two B.U.T. 6-cyl. horizontal type of 150 b.h.p.

Transmission
Mechanical. Standard

Body: 64′ × 6″ × 9′ 3″. Gangwayed both ends, side driving compartment at one end

Weight: 38 tons **Seats:** 2nd, 64

SC50936

Derby Works, B.R. (2)
MOTOR BRAKE SECOND ■

Introduced: 1959

Engines
Two B.U.T. (Leyland) 6-cyl. horizontal type of 150 b.h.p.

Transmission
Mechanical. Standard

Body: 57′ 6″ × 9′ 2″ **Weight:** 28 tons 10 cwt **Seats:** 2nd, 52

M50938	M50947	M50956	M50964	M50972	M50980
M50939	M50948	M50957	M50965	M50973	M50981
M50940	M50949	M50958	M50966	M50974	M50982
M50941	M50950	M50959	M50967	M50975	M50983
M50942	M50951	M50960	M50968	M50976	M50984
M50943	M50952	M50961	M50969	M50977	M50985
M50944	M50953	M50962	M50970	M50978	M50986
M50945	M50954	M50963	M50971	M50979	M50987
M50946	M50955				

Derby Works, B.R. (3 Suburban)
MOTOR SECOND ★

Introduced: 1958

Engines
Two Rolls-Royce horizontal type of 238 b.h.p.

Transmission
Hydraulic. Twin-disc torque converter

Body: 64′ 0″ × 9′ 3″. Non-gangwayed, side doors to each seating bay

Weight: 39 tons 10 cwt **Seats:** 2nd, 95

E50988	E50992	E50996	E50999	E51002	E51005
E50989	E50993	E50997	E51000	E51003	E51006
E50990	E50994	E50998	E51001	E51004	E51007
E50991	E50995				

Swindon Works, B.R. (6 Inter-City)
MOTOR SECOND (L) ●

Introduced: 1959

Engines
Two B.U.T. 6-cyl. horizontal type of 150 b.h.p.

Transmission
Mechanical. Standard

Body: 64' 6" × 9' 3". Gangwayed both ends, side driving compartment one end

Weight: 38 tons   **Seats:** 2nd, 64

SC51008	SC51012	SC51016	SC51020	SC51024	SC51027
SC51009	SC51013	SC51017	SC51021	SC51025	SC51028
SC51010	SC51014	SC51018	SC51022	SC51026	SC51029
SC51011	SC51015	SC51019	SC51023		

Swindon Works, B.R. (3 or 6 Inter-City)
MOTOR BRAKE SECOND (L) ●

Introduced: 1959

Engines
Two B.U.T. (A.E.C.) 6-cyl. horizontal type of 150 b.h.p.

Transmission
Mechanical. Standard

Body: 64' 6" × 9' 3"   **Weight:** 38 tons   **Seats:** 2nd, 52

SC51030	SC51034	SC51038	SC51042	SC51046	SC51049
SC51031	SC51035	SC51039	SC51043	SC51047	SC51050
SC51032	SC51036	SC51040	SC51044	SC51048	SC51051
SC51033	SC51037	SC51041	SC51045		

Gloucester R. C. & W. Co. (3 Cross Country)
MOTOR BRAKE COMPOSITE ■

Introduced: 1958

Engines
Two B.U.T. (A.E.C.) 6-cyl. horizontal type of 150 b.h.p.

Transmission
Mechanical. Standard

Body: 64' 6" × 9' 3"   **Weight:** 36 tons 19 cwt   **Seats:** 1st, 18; 2nd, 16

W51052	M51057	M51062	M51067	M51072	M 51076
W51053	M51058	M51063	M51068	M51073	W51077
W51054	M51059	M51064	M51069	M51074	W51078
W51055	M51060	M51065	M51070	M51075	W51079
W51056	M51061	M51066	M51071		

Gloucester R. C. & W. Co. (3 Cross Country)
MOTOR SECOND (L) ■
Introduced: 1958

Engines
Two B.U.T. (A.E.C.) 6-cyl. horizontal
type of 150 b.h.p.

Transmission
Mechanical. Standard

Body: 64' 6" × 9' 3"   **Weight:** 37 tons 10 cwt   **Seats:** 2nd, 68

W51080	M51085	M51090	M51095	M51100	M 51104
W51081	M51086	M51091	M51096	M51101	W51105
W51082	M51087	M51092	M51097	M51102	W51106
W51083	M51088	M51093	M51098	M51103	W51107
W51084	M51089	M51094	M51099		

Gloucester R. C. & W. Co. (2)
MOTOR BRAKE SECOND ■
Introduced: 1957

For details see SC50339-M50357

SC51108	SC51112	SC51116	SC51119	SC51122	SC51125
SC51109		SC51117	SC51120	SC51123	SC51126
SC51110	SC51114	SC51118	SC51121	SC51124	SC51127
SC51111	SC51115				

Derby Works, B.R. (3 Suburban)
MOTOR BRAKE SECOND ■
Introduced: 1958

For details see M50050-W50091

W51128	M51131	M 51133	W51135	W51137	W51139
M 51129	M51132	W51134	W51136	W51138	W51140
M 51130					

Derby Works, B.R. (3 Suburban)
MOTOR SECOND ■
Introduced: 1958

For details see M50092-W50133

W51141	M51144	M 51146	W51148	W51150	W51152
M 51142	M51145	W51147	W51149	W51151	W51153
M 51143					

Derby Works, B.R. (3 Suburban)
MOTOR BRAKE SECOND ★
Introduced: 1958

Engines
Two Rolls-Royce horizontal type of
238 b.h.p.

Transmission
Hydraulic. Twin-disc torque converter

Body: 64' 0" × 9' 3". Non-gangwayed, side doors to each seating bay
Weight: 39 tons 10 cwt   **Seats:** 2nd, 65

E51154	E51158	E51162	E51165	E51168	E51171
E51155	E51159	E51163	E51166	E51169	E51172
E51156	E51160	E51164	E51167	E51170	E51173
E51157	E51161				

Metropolitan-Cammell (2)

MOTOR BRAKE SECOND ■

Introduced: 1958
Engines
Two B.U.T. (A.E.C.) 6-cyl. horizontal
type of 150 b.h.p.

Transmission
Mechanical. Standard

Body: 57: 0″ × 9′ 3″　　　**Weight:** 32 tons　　　**Seats:** 2nd, 52

M51174	M51188	M51202	NE51215	SC51228	SC51241
M51175	M51189	M51203	NE51216	SC51229	SC51242
M51176	M51190	NE51204	NE51217	SC51230	SC51243
M51177	M51191	NE51205	NE51218	SC51231	SC51244
M51178	M51192	NE51206	NE51219	SC51232	SC51245
M51179	M51193	NE51207	NE51220	SC51233	SC51246
M51180	M51194	NE51208	NE51221	SC51234	SC51247
M51181	M51195	NE51209	NE51222	SC51235	SC51248
M51182	M51196	NE51210	NE51223	SC51236	SC51249
M51183	M51197	NE51211	SC51224	SC51237	SC51250
M51184	M51198	NE51212	SC51225	SC51238	SC51251
M51185	M51199	NE51213	SC51226	SC51239	SC51252
M51186	M51200	NE51214	SC51227	SC51240	SC51253
M51187	M51201				

Cravens (2)

MOTOR BRAKE SECOND ■

Introduced: 1958
Engines
Two B.U.T. (A.E.C.) 6-cyl. horizontal
type of 150 b.h.p.

Transmission
Mechanical. Standard

Body: 57′ 6″ × 9′ 2″　　　**Weight:** 30 tons　　　**Seats:** 2nd, 52

E51254	E51262	E51270	E51278	E51286	E51294
E51255	E51263	E51271	E51279	E51287	E51295
E51256		E51272	E51280	E51288	E51296
E51257	E51265	E51273	E51281	E51289	E51297
E51258	E51266	E51274	E51282	E51290	E51298
E51259	E51267	E51275	E51283	E51291	E51299
E51260	E51268	E51276	E51284	E51292	E51300
E51261	E51269	E51277	E51285	E51293	E51301

Birmingham R. C. & W. Co. (3 Suburban)

MOTOR BRAKE SECOND ■

Introduced: 1960
Engines

Transmission
Mechanical. Standard

Body: 64′ 0″ × 9′ 3″. Non-gangwayed, side doors to each seating bay
Weight: 36 tons　　　**Seats:** 2nd, 65

Gloucester 3-car cross-country unit on a Portsmouth–Bristol working [*J. H. Bird*

Cravens motor brake second No. E51270 on a Kings Cross–Baldock working
[*D. L. Percival*

Pressed Steel motor second No. W51379 at Southall [*D. L. Percival*

W51302	W51305	W51308	W51311	W51313	W51315
W51303	W51306	W51309	W51312	W51314	W51316
W51304	W51307	W51310			

Birmingham R. C. & W. Co. (3 Suburban)
MOTOR SECOND ∎

Introduced: 1960

Engines

Transmission
Mechanical. Standard

Body: 64′ 0″ × 9′ 3″. Non-gangwayed, side doors to each seating bay

Weight: 36 tons   **Seats: 2nd,** 91

W51317	W51320	W51323	W51326	W51328	W51330
W51318	W51321	W51324	W51327	W51329	W51331
W51319	W51322	W51325			

Pressed Steel Co. (3 Suburban)
MOTOR BRAKE SECOND ∎

Introduced: 1959

Engines
Two B.U.T. (Leyland) 6-cyl. horizontal type of 150 b.h.p.

Transmission
Mechanical. Standard

Body: 64′ 0″ × 9′ 3″. Non-gangwayed, side doors to each seating bay

Weight: 36 tons   **Seats: 2nd,** 65

W51332	W51339	W51346	W51353	W51360	W51367
W51333	W51340	W51347	W51354	W51361	W51368
W51334	W51341	W51348	W51355	W51362	W51369
W51335	W51342	W51349	W51356	W51363	W51370
W51336	W51343	W51350	W51357	W51364	W51371
W51337	W51344	W51351	W51358	W51365	W51372
W51338	W51345	W51352	W51359	W51366	W51373

Pressed Steel Co. (3 Suburban)
MOTOR SECOND ∎

Introduced: 1959

Engines
Two B.U.T. (Leyland) 6-cyl. horizontal type of 150 b.h.p.

Transmission
Mechanical. Standard

Body: 64′ 0″ × 9′ 3″. Non-gangwayed, side doors to each seating bay

Weight: 36 tons   **Seats: 2nd,** 91

W51374	W51381	W51388	W51395	W51402	W51409
W51375	W51382	W51389	W51396	W51403	W51410
W51376	W51383	W51390	W51397	W51404	W51411
W51377	W51384	W51391	W51398	W51405	W51412
W51378	W51385	W51392	W51399	W51406	W51413
W51379	W51386	W51393	W51400	W51407	W51414
W51380	W51387	W51394	W51401	W51408	W51415

Derby Works, B.R. (2)
MOTOR BRAKE SECOND ■

Introduced: 1960

Engines
Two B.U.T. (Leyland) 6-cyl. horizontal type of 150 b.h.p.

Transmission
Mechanical. Standard

Body: 57′ 6″ × 9′ 2″ **Weight:** 29 tons **Seats: 2nd,** 52

M51416	M51418	M51420	M51422	M51423	M51424
M51417	M51419	M51421			

Metropolitan-Cammell (2)
MOTOR BRAKE SECOND ■

Introduced: 1959

Engines
Two B.U.T. (Leyland) 6-cyl. horizontal type of 150 b.h.p.

Transmission
Mechanical. Standard

Body: 57′ 0″ × 9′ 3″ **Weight:** 32 tons **Seats: 2nd,** 52

NE51425	NE51427	NE51429	NE51431	NE51433	NE51434
NE51426	NE51428	NE51430	NE51432		

Metropolitan-Cammell (3 or 4*)
MOTOR BRAKE SECOND ■

Introduced: 1959

Engines
Two B.U.T. (Leyland) 6-cyl. horizontal type of 150 b.h.p.

Transmission
Mechanical. Standard

Body: 57′ 0″ × 9′ 3″ **Weight:** 32 tons **Seats: 2nd,** 52

NE51435*	NE51441*	SC51447	SC51453	SC51459	SC51465
NE51436*	NE51442*	SC51448	SC51454	SC51460	SC51466
NE51437*	NE51443*	SC51449	SC51455	SC51461	SC51467
NE51438*	NE51444	SC51450	SC51456	SC51462	SC51468
NE51439*	SC51445	SC51451	SC51457	SC51463	SC51469
NE51440*	SC51446	SC51452	SC51458	SC51464	SC51470

Cravens (2)
MOTOR BRAKE SECOND ■

Introduced: 1959

Engines
Two B.U.T. (A.E.C.) 6-cyl. horizontal type of 150 b.h.p.

Transmission
Mechanical. Standard

Body: 57′ 6″ × 9′ 2″ **Weight:** 30 tons 10 cwt **Seats: 2nd,** 52

E51471	SC51475	SC51479	SC51483	SC51487	SC51491
E51472	SC51476	SC51480	SC51484	SC51488	SC51492
SC51473	SC51477	SC51481	SC51485	SC51489	SC51493
SC51474	SC51478	SC51482	SC51486	SC51490	SC51494

Metropolitan-Cammell (2)
MOTOR COMPOSITE (L) ∎

Introduced: 1959

Engines
Two B.U.T. (Leyland) 6-cyl. horizontal type of 150 b.h.p.

Transmission
Mechanical. Standard

Body: 57' 0" × 9' 3"   **Weight:** 32 tons   **Seats:** 1st, 12; 2nd, 53

NE51495	NE51497	NE51499	NE51501	NE51503	NE51504
NE51496	NE51498	NE51500	NE51502

Metropolitan-Cammell (3 or 4*)
MOTOR COMPOSITE (L) ∎

Introduced: 1959

Engines
Two B.U.T. (Leyland) 6-cyl. horizontal type of 150 b.h.p.

Transmission
Mechanical. Standard

Body: 57' 0" × 9' 3"   **Weight:** 32 tons   **Seats:** 1st, 12; 2nd, 53

NE51505*	NE51511*	SC51517	SC51523	SC51529	SC51535
NE51506*	NE51512*	SC51518	SC51524	SC51530	SC51536
NE51507*	NE51513*	SC51519	SC51525	SC51531	SC51537
NE51508*	NE51514*	SC51520	SC51526	SC51532	SC51538
NE51509*	SC51515	SC51521	SC51527	SC51533	SC51539
NE51510*	SC51516	SC51522	SC51528	SC51534	SC51540

Metropolitan-Cammell (3)
MOTOR BRAKE SECOND ∎

Introduced: 1959

For details see NE51435-SC51470

NE51541	NE51543	NE51544	NE51545	NE51546	NE51547
NE51542

Metropolitan-Cammell (2)
MOTOR BRAKE SECOND ∎

Introduced: 1960

Engines
Two B.U.T. (A.E.C.) 6-cyl. horizontal type of 150 b.h.p.

Transmission
Mechanical. Standard

Body: 57' 0" × 9' 3"   **Weight:** 31 tons 10 cwt   **Seats:** 2nd, 52

NE51548   NE51549   NE51550

Metropolitan-Cammell (3)
MOTOR COMPOSITE (L) ∎

Introduced: 1960

For details see NE51505-SC51540

NE51551	NE51553	NE51554	NE51555	NE51556	NE51557
NE51552

Metropolitan-Cammell (2)
MOTOR COMPOSITE (L) ■

Introduced: 1960
Engines
Two B.U.T. (A.E.C.) 6-cyl. horizontal
type of 150 b.h.p.

Transmission
Mechanical. Standard

Body: 57′ 0″ × 9′ 3″   **Weight:** 31 tons 10 cwt   **Seats:** 1st, 12; 2nd, 53

NE51558	NE51559	NE51560

Derby Works, B.R. (2)
MOTOR COMPOSITE (L) ■

Introduced: 1959
Engines
Two B.U.T. (Leyland) 6-cyl. horizon-
tal type of 150 b.h.p.

Transmission
Mechanical. Standard

Body: 57′ 6″ × 9′ 2″   **Weight:** 27 tons   **Seats:** 1st, 12; 2nd, 53

M51561	M51563	M51565	M51567	M51569	M51571
M51562	M51564	M51566	M51568	M51570	M51572

Swindon Works, B.R. (3 Cross Country)
MOTOR BRAKE COMPOSITE (L) ■

Introduced: 1961
Engines
Two B.U.T. 6-cyl. horizontal type of
150 b.h.p.

Transmission
Mechanical. Standard

Body: 64′ 6″ × 9′ 3″   **Weight:** 36 tons 7 cwt   **Seats:** 1st, 18; 2nd, 16

W51573	W51575	W51577	W51579	W51580	W51581
W51574	W51576	W51578			

Swindon Works, B.R. (3 Cross Country)
MOTOR SECOND (L) ■

Introduced: 1961
Engines
Two B.U.T. 6-cyl. horizontal type of
150 b.h.p.

Transmission
Mechanical. Standard

Body: 64′ 6″ × 9′ 3″   **Weight:** 36 tons 10 cwt   **Seats:** 2nd, 68

W51582	W51584	W51586	W51588	W51589	W51590
W51583	W51585	W51587			

Derby Works, B.R. (4 Suburban)
MOTOR BRAKE SECOND ■

Introduced: 1959
Engines
Two Rolls-Royce 8-cyl. horizontal
type of 238 b.h.p.

Transmission
Hydraulic. Torque converter

Body: 64′ 0″ × 9′ 3″. Non-gangwayed, side doors to each seating bay

Weight: 40 tons   **Seats:** 2nd, 76

M51591	M51601	M51612	M51622	M51632	M51642
M51592	M51602	M51613	M51623	M51633	M51643
M51593	M51603	M51614	M51624	M51634	M51644
	M51604	M51615	M51625	M51635	M51645
M51595	M51605	M51616	M51626	M51636	M51646
M51596	M51606	M51617	M51627	M51637	M51647
M51597	M51607	M51618	M51628	M51638	M51648
M51598	M51608	M51619	M51629	M51639	M51649
M51599	M51610	M51620	M51630	M51640	M51650
M51600	M51611	M51621	M51631	M51641	

Derby Works, B.R.   (4 Suburban)
MOTOR BRAKE SECOND   ■

Introduced: 1960

Engines
Two B.U.T. (Leyland Albion) 6-cyl.
horizontal type of 230 b.h.p.

Transmission
Mechanical. Standard

Body: 64′ 0″ × 9′ 3″. Non-gangwayed, side doors to each seating bay

Weight: 38 tons   **Seats:** 2nd, 78

M51651	M51656	M51661	M51666	M51671	M51676
M51652	M51657	M51662	M51667	M51672	M51677
M51653	M51658	M51663	M51668	M51673	M51678
M51654	M51659	M51664	M51669	M51674	M51679
M51655	M51660	M51665	M51670	M51675	M51680

Cravens   (2)
MOTOR BRAKE SECOND   ■

Introduced: 1959

Engine
One Rolls-Royce 8-cyl. horizontal
type of 238 b.h.p.

Transmission
Mechanical. Standard

Body: 57′ 6″ × 9′ 2″   **Weight:** 29 tons 10 cwt   **Seats:** 2nd, 52

M51681	M51686	M51690	M51694	M51698	M51702
M51682	M51687	M51691	M51695	M51699	M51703
M51683	M51688	M51692	M51696	M51700	M51704
M51684	M51689	M51693	M51697	M51701	M51705
M51685					

Cravens   (2)
MOTOR COMPOSITE (L)   ■

Introduced: 1959

Engine
One Rolls-Royce 8-cyl. horizontal
type of 238 b.h.p.

Transmission
Mechanical. Standard

Body: 57′ 6″ × 9′ 2″   **Weight:** 29 tons   **Seats:** 1st, 12; 2nd, 51

M51706	M51711	M51715	M51719	M51723	M51727
M51707	M51712	M51716	M51720	M51724	M51728
M51708	M51713	M51717	M51721	M51725	M51729
M51709	M51714	M51718	M51722	M51726	M51730
M51710					

Cravens (2)
MOTOR BRAKE SECOND ∎

Introduced: 1959

Engine
One Rolls-Royce 8-cyl. horizontal type of 238 b.h.p.

Transmission
Hydraulic. Torque converter

Body: 57′ 6″ × 9′ 2″   **Weight:** 29 tons 10 cwt   **Seats: 2nd, 52**

M51731	M51736	M51740	M51744	M51748	M51752
M51732	M51737	M51741	M51745	M51749	M51753
M51733	M51738	M51742	M51746	M51750	M51754
M51734	M51739	M51743	M51747	M51751	M51755
M51735					

Cravens (2)
MOTOR COMPOSITE (L) ∎

Introduced: 1959

Engine
One Rolls-Royce 8-cyl. horizontal type of 238 b.h.p.

Transmission
Hydraulic. Torque converter

Body: 57′ 6″ × 9′ 2″   **Weight:** 29 tons   **Seats: 1st, 12; 2nd, 51**

M51756	M51760	M51765	M51769	M51774	M51777
M51757	M51761	M51766	M51771	M51775	M51778
M51758	M51762	M51767	M51772	M51776	M51779
M51759	M51764	M51768	M51773		

Swindon Works, B.R. (3 Cross Country)
MOTOR BRAKE COMPOSITE ∎

Introduced: 1959

Engines
Two B.U.T. 6-cyl. horizontal type of 150 b.h.p.

Transmission
Mechanical. Standard

Body: 64′ 6″ × 9′ 3″   **Weight:** 36 tons 7 cwt   **Seats: 1st, 18; 2nd, 16**

| SC51781 | SC51783 | SC51784 | SC51785 | SC51786 | SC51787 |
| SC51782 | | | | | |

Swindon Works, B.R. (3 Cross Country)
MOTOR SECOND (L) ∎

Introduced: 1960

Engines
Two B.U.T. 6-cyl horizontal type of 150 b.h.p.

Transmission
Mechanical. Standard

Body: 64′ 6″ × 9′ 3″   **Weight:** 36 tons 10 cwt   **Seats: 2nd, 68**

| SC51788 | SC51790 | SC51791 | SC51792 | SC51793 | SC51794 |
| SC51789 | | | | | |

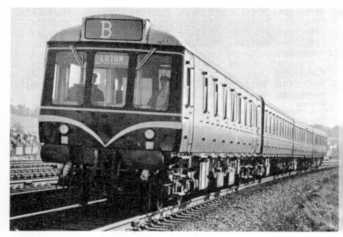

Derby 4-car suburban unit on a St. Pancras–Luton working　　　　　　[*British Railways*

Birmingham R.C. & W. Co. 3-car units approaching Todmorden　　　[*I. G. Holt*

Metropolitan-Cammell (3)

MOTOR BRAKE SECOND ■

Introduced: 1959

Engines
Two B.U.T. (A.E.C.) 6-cyl. horizontal type of 150 b.h.p.

Transmission
Mechanical. Standard

Body: 57' 0" × 9' 3"   **Weight:** 32 tons   **Seats:** 2nd, 52

SC51795	SC51797	SC51798	SC51799	SC51800	SC51801
SC51796					

Metropolitan-Cammell (3)

MOTOR COMPOSITE (L) ■

Introduced: 1959

Engines
Two B.U.T. (A.E.C.) 6-cyl. horizontal type of 150 b.h.p.

Transmission
Mechanical. Standard

Body: 57' 0" × 9' 3"   **Weight:** 32 tons   **Seats:** 1st, 12; 2nd, 53

SC51802	SC51804	SC51805	SC51806	SC51807	SC51808
SC51803					

Birmingham R. C. & W. Co. (3)

MOTOR BRAKE COMPOSITE ■

Introduced: 1961

Engines
Two Rolls-Royce Series 130D of 180 b.h.p.

Transmission
Mechanical. Standard

Body: 57' 6" × 9' 3"   **Weight:** 32 tons   **Seats:** 1st, 12; 2nd, 33

NE51809	NE51813	NE51816	NE51819	NE51823	NE51826
NE51810	NE51814	NE51817	NE51820	NE51824	NE51827
NE51811	NE51815	NE51818	NE51822	NE51825	NE51828
NE51812					

Birmingham R. C. & W. Co. (3)

MOTOR COMPOSITE (L) ■

Introduced: 1961

Engines
Two Rolls-Royce Series 130D of 180 b.h.p.

Transmission
Mechanical. Standard

Body: 57' 6" × 9' 3"   **Weight:** 31 tons 10 cwt   **Seats:** 1st, 12; 2nd, 54

NE51829	NE51833	NE51836	NE51840	NE51843	NE51846
NE51830	NE51834	NE51838	NE51841	NE51844	NE51847
NE51831	NE51835	NE51839	NE51842	NE51845	NE51848
NE51832					

Derby 4-car suburban unit on an Aylesbury–Marylebone working [B. *Stephenson*

Swindon motor composite No. NE51963 of a 6-car Trans-Pennine unit [D. L. *Percival*

Derby twin unit with motor composite No. M52042 leading [M. *Mensing*

140

Derby Works, B.R.
MOTOR BRAKE SECOND
(4 Suburban) ■

Introduced: 1960

Engines
Two B.U.T. (Leyland Albion) 6-cyl. horizontal type of 230 b.h.p.

Transmission
Mechanical. Standard

Body: 64' 0" × 9' 3". Non-gangwayed, side doors to each seating bay

Weight: 38 tons

Seats: 2nd, 78

M51849	M51858	M51867	M51876	M51885	M51893
M51850	M51859	M51868	M51877	M51886	M51894
M51851	M51860	M51869	M51878	M51887	M51895
M51852	M51861	M51870	M51879	M51888	M51896
M51853	M51862	M51871	M51880	M51889	M51897
M51854	M51863	M51872	M51881	M51890	M51898
M51855	M51864	M51873	M51882	M51891	M51899
M51856	M51865	M51874	M51883	M51892	M51900
M51857	M51866	M51875	M51884		

Derby Works, B.R.
MOTOR BRAKE SECOND
(2) ■

Introduced: 1960

Engines
Two B.U.T. (Leyland) 6-cyl. horizontal type of 150 b.h.p.

Transmission
Mechanical. Standard

Body: 57' 6" × 9' 2"   **Weight:** 28 tons 10 cwt   **Seats: 2nd,** 52

M51901	M51910	M51918	M51926	M51934	M51942
M51902	M51911	M51919	M51927	M51935	M51943
M51903	M51912	M51920	M51928	M51936	M51945
M51904	M51913	M51921	M51929	M51937	M51946
M51905	M51914	M51922	M51930	M51938	M51947
M51906	M51915	M51923	M51931	M51939	M51948
M51907	M51916	M51924	M51932	M51940	M51949
M51908	M51917	M51925	M51933	M51941	M51950
M51909					

Swindon Works, B.R.
MOTOR COMPOSITE
(6 Trans-Pennine) ■

Introduced: 1960

Engines
Two B.U.T. (Leyland) 6-cyl. horizontal type of 230 b.h.p.

Transmission
Mechanical. Standard

Body: 64' 6" × 9' 3"   **Weight:**   **Seats: 1st,** 21; **2nd,** 36

NE51951	NE51954	NE51957	NE51960	NE51963	NE51966
NE51952	NE51955	NE51958	NE51961	NE51964	NE51967
NE51953	NE51956	NE51959	NE51962	NE51965	

Swindon Works, B.R.
MOTOR BRAKE SECOND (K)
(non-driving)

Introduced: 1960

Engines
Two B.U.T. (Leyland) 6-cyl. horizontal type of 230 b.h.p.

Transmission
Mechanical. Standard

Body: 64' 6" × 9' 3"   **Weight:**   **Seats: 2nd,** 48

NE51968	NE51971	NE51974	NE51977	NE51980	NE51983
NE51969	NE51972	NE51975	NE51978	NE51981	NE51984
NE51970	NE51973	NE51976	NE51979	NE51982	

Derby Works, B.R.   (3)
MOTOR BRAKE SECOND   ■

Introduced: 1960

Engines
Two B.U.T. 6-cyl. horizontal type of 150 b.h.p.

Transmission
Mechanical. Standard

Body: 58' 1" × 9' 3"   **Weight:** 34 tons 10 cwt   **Seats: 2nd,** 52

SC51985	SC51990	SC51995	SC51999	SC52003	SC52007
SC51986	SC51991	SC51996	SC52000	SC52004	SC52008
SC51987	SC51992	SC51997	SC52001	SC52005	SC52009
SC51988	SC51993	SC51998	SC52002	SC52006	SC52010
SC51989	SC51994				

Derby Works, B.R.   (3)
MOTOR COMPOSITE (L)   ■

Introduced: 1960

Engines
Two B.U.T. 6-cyl. horizontal type of 150 b.h.p.

Transmission
Mechanical. Standard

Body: 58' 1" × 9' 3"   **Weight:** 35 tons   **Seats: 1st,** 12; **2nd,** 53

SC52011	SC52016	SC52021	SC52025	SC52029	SC52033
SC52012	SC52017	SC52022	SC52026	SC52030	SC52034
SC52013	SC52018	SC52023	SC52027	SC52031	SC52035
SC52014	SC52019	SC52024	SC52028	SC52032	SC52036
SC52015	SC52020				

Derby Works, B.R.   (2)
MOTOR COMPOSITE (L)   ■

Introduced: 1960

Engines
Two B.U.T. (Leyland) 6-cyl. horizontal type of 150 b.h.p.

Transmission
Mechanical. Standard

Body: 57' 6" × 9' 2"   **Weight:** 28 tons   **Seats: 1st,** 12; **2nd,** 53

M52037	M52042	M52047	M52052	M52057	M52062
M52038	M52043	M52048	M52053	M52058	M52063
M52039	M52044	M52049	M52054	M52059	M52064
M52040	M52045	M52050	M52055	M52060	M52065
M52041	M52046	M52051	M52056	M52061	

Birmingham R. C. & W. Co. (3)
MOTOR BRAKE COMPOSITE ■

Introduced: 1961
Engines
Two Rolls-Royce Series 130D of 180 b.h.p.

Transmission
Mechanical, Standard

Body: 57′ 6″ × 9′ 3″   **Weight:** 32 tons   **Seats:** 1st, 12; 2nd, 33

M52066	M52068	M52070	M52072	M52074	M52075
M52067	M52069	M52071	M52073		

Birmingham R. C. & W. Co. (3)
MOTOR COMPOSITE (L) ■

Introduced: 1961
Engines
Two Rolls-Royce Series 130D of 180 b.h.p.

Transmission
Mechanical, Standard

Body: 57′ 6″ × 9′ 3″   **Weight:** 31 tons 10 cwt   **Seats:** 1st, 12; 2nd, 54

M52076	M52078	M52080	M52082	M52084	M52085
M52077	M52079	M52081	M52083		

Swindon Works, B.R. (4 Inter-City)
MOTOR BRAKE SECOND (L) ■

Introduced: 1963
Engines
Two B.U.T. (Leyland) 6-cyl. horizontal type of 230 b.h.p.

Transmission
Mechanical, Standard

Body: 64′ 11½″ × 9′ 3″   **Weight:** 41 tons   **Seats:** 2nd, 32

W52086	W52088	W52090	W52092	W52094	W52095
W52087	W52089	W52091	W52093		

Swindon Works, B.R. (4 Inter-City)
MOTOR SECOND (K) ■

Introduced: 1963
Engines
Two B.U.T. (Leyland) 6-cyl. horizontal type of 230 b.h.p.

Transmission
Mechanical, Standard

Body: 64′ 11½″ × 9′ 3″   **Weight:** 42 tons   **Seats:** 2nd, 56

W52096	W52098	W52100	W52102	W52104	W52105
W52097	W52099	W52101	W52103		

Swindon 4-car inter-city unit with motor second No. W52097 leading on a Portsmouth–Cardiff working

[J. H. Bird

Pressed Steel motor brake second No. W55027 at Oxford

[M. York

Gloucester R.C. & W. Co. motor parcels van No. M55993 at Walsall

[A. J. Wheeler

Gloucester R. C. & W. Co. (1)

MOTOR BRAKE SECOND ■

Introduced: 1958
Engines
Two B.U.T. (A.E.C.) 6-cyl. horizontal
type of 150 b.h.p.

Transmission
Mechanical. Standard

Body: 64′ 6″ × 9′ 3″. Non-gangwayed, side doors to each seating bay

Weight: 35 tons   **Seats: 2nd,** 65

W55000	M55004	M55008	W55011	W55014	W55017
W55001	M55005	M55009	M 55012	W55015	M 55018
M 55002	M55006	M55010	W55013	W55016	W55019
M 55003	M55007				

Pressed Steel Co. (1)

MOTOR BRAKE SECOND ■

Introduced: 1960
Engines
Two B.U.T. 6-cyl. horizontal type of
150 b.h.p.

Transmission
Mechanical. Standard

Body: 64′ 6″ × 9′ 3″. Non-gangwayed, side doors to each seating bay

Weight: 37 tons   **Seats: 2nd,** 65

W55020	W55023	W55026	W55029	W55032	W55034
W55021	W55024	W55027	W55030	W55033	W55035
W55022	W55025	W55028	W55031		

Gloucester R. C. & W. Co. (1)

MOTOR PARCELS VAN ■

Introduced: 1959
Engines
Two B.U.T. (Leyland Albion) 6-cyl.
horizontal type of 230 b.h.p.

Transmission
Mechanical. Standard

Body: 64′ 6″ × 9′ 3″ (Non-gangwayed*)   **Weight:** 41 tons (40 tons*)

M55987*	M55989*	W55991	M55993	M55995	M55996
M55988*	M55990*	W55992	M55994		

Cravens (1)

MOTOR PARCELS VAN ◆

Introduced: 1958
Engines
Two B.U.T. (A.E.C.) 6-cyl. horizontal
type of 150 b.h.p.

Transmission
Mechanical. Standard

Body: 57′ 6″ × 9′ 3″. Non-gangwayed   **Weight:** 30 tons

M55997	M55998	M55999

Derby Works, B.R. (2)
DRIVING TRAILER COMPOSITE (L) ∎

Introduced: 1956
Body: 64′ 6″ × 9′ 3″   **Weight:** 29 tons (31 tons*)   **Seats:** 1st, 12; 2nd, 62

E56001*	E56009*	E56017	E56025	E56033	E56041
E56002	E56010	E56018	E56026	E56034	E56042
E56003	E56011	E56019	E56027*	E56035	E56043
E56004*	E56012	E56020	E56028	E56036	E56044
E56005*	E56013	E56021	E56029	E56037	E56045
E56006	E56014	E56022	E56030	E56038	E56047
E56007*	E56015	E56023*	E56031	E56039	E56048
E56008*	E56016	E56024	E56032	E56040	E56049

Metropolitan-Cammell (2)
DRIVING TRAILER COMPOSITE (L) ∎

Introduced: 1957
Body: 57′ 0″ × 9′ 3″   **Weight:** 25 tons   **Seats:** 1st, 12; 2nd, 53

NE56050	M56058	NE56066	NE56073	M56080	NE56087
NE56051	NE56059	NE56067	NE56074	NE56081	NE56088
NE56052	M56060	NE56068	NE56075	NE56082	NE56089
NE56053	NE56061	NE56069	NE56076	NE56083	NE56090
E56054	NE56062	NE56070	NE56077	NE56084	NE56091
M56055	NE56063	NE56071	NE56078	NE56085	NE56092
NE56056	NE56064	NE56072	NE56079	NE56086	NE56093
NE56057	NE56065				

Gloucester R. C. & W. Co. (2)
DRIVING TRAILER COMPOSITE (L) ∎

Introduced: 1957
Body: 57′ 6″ × 9′ 3″   **Weight:** 25 tons   **Seats:** 1st, 12; 2nd, 54

SC56094	SC56098	SC56102	M56105	M56108	M56111
SC56095	SC56099	M56103	M56106	M56109	M56112
SC56096	SC56100	M56104	M56107	M56110	M56113
SC56097	SC56101				

Cravens (2)
DRIVING TRAILER COMPOSITE (L) ∎

Introduced: 1956
Body: 57′ 6″ × 9′ 2″   **Weight:** 23 tons   **Seats:** 1st, 12; 2nd, 51 (54*)

Right: Park Royal twin unit on a Walsall–Dudley working
[*M. Mensing*

Centre: Wickham driving trailer composite No. E56172
[*D. L. Percival*

Bottom: Birmingham R.C. & W. Co. driving trailer composite No. M56178
[*P. J. Sharpe*

NE56114	NE56120	NE56126	E56132	E56138	NE56144
E56115	E56121	NE56127	NE56133	E56139	M56145*
NE56116	NE56122	NE56128	NE56134	NE56140	M56146*
E56117	NE56123	NE56129	NE56135	NE56141	M56147*
NE56118	NE56124	NE56130	NE56136	NE56142	M56148*
NE56119	NE56125	E56131	NE56137	NE56143	M56149*

Park Royal Vehicles (2)
DRIVING TRAILER COMPOSITE (L) ■

Introduced: 1957
Body: 57′ 6″ × 9′ 3″   **Weight:** 26 tons 7 cwt   **Seats:** 1st, 16; 2nd, 48

M56150	M56154	M56158	M56161	M56164	M56167
M56151	M56155	M56159	M56162	M56165	M56168
M56152	M56156	M56160	M56163	M56166	M56169
M56153	M56157				

D. Wickham & Co. (2)
DRIVING TRAILER COMPOSITE (L) ■

Introduced: 1957
Body: 57′ 6″ × 9′ 3″   **Weight:** 20 tons 10 cwt   **Seats:** 1st, 16; 2nd, 50

E56172	E56173

Birmingham R. C. & W. Co. (2)
DRIVING TRAILER COMPOSITE (L) ■

Introduced: 1958
Body: 57′ 6″ × 9′ 3″   **Weight:**   **Seats:** 1st, 12; 2nd, 54

M56175	M56177	M56179	M56181	M56183	M56184
M56176	M56178	M56180	M56182		

Birmingham R. C. & W. Co. (2)
DRIVING TRAILER COMPOSITE (L) ■

Introduced: 1958
Body: 57′ 6″ × 9′ 3″   **Weight:** 24 tons   **Seats:** 1st, 12; 2nd, 54

NE56185	NE56186	NE56187	NE56188	NE56189

Derby Works, B.R. (2)
DRIVING TRAILER COMPOSITE (L)

Introduced: 1958
Body: 57′ 6″ × 9′ 2″   **Weight:** 22 tons   **Seats:** 1st, 12; 2nd, 53

NE56190	NE56195	NE56200	NE56204	NE56208	M56212
NE56191	NE56196	E56201	NE56205	NE56209	M56213
NE56192	NE56197	E56202	NE56206	NE56210	M56214
NE56193	NE56198	NE56203	NE56207	M56211	M56215
NE56194	NE56199				

Metropolitan-Cammell (2)
DRIVING TRAILER COMPOSITE (L) ■

Introduced: 1957
Body: 57′ 0″ × 9′ 3″   **Weight:** 25 tons   **Seats:** 1st, 12; 2nd, 45

  NE56218   NE56219   NE56220

Derby Works, B.R. (2)
DRIVING TRAILER COMPOSITE (L) ■

Introduced: 1959
Body: 57′ 6″ × 9′ 2″   **Weight:** 22 tons   **Seats:** 1st, 12; 2nd, 53

M56221	M56232	M56242	M56252	M56262	M56271
M56222	M56233	M56243	M56253	M56263	M56272
M56223	M56234	M56244	M56254	M56264	M56273
M56224	M56235	M56245	M56255	M56265	M56274
M56225	M56236	M56246	M56256	M56266	M56275
M56226	M56237	M56247	M56257	M56267	M56276
M56227	M56238	M56248	M56258	M56268	M56277
M56228	M56239	M56249	M56259	M56269	M56278
M56229	M56240	M56250	M56260	M56270	M56279
M56230	M56241	M56251	M56261		
M56231					

Pressed Steel Co. (2)
DRIVING TRAILER SECOND ■

(For use with Single Unit cars Nos. W55000-35)
Introduced: 1960
Body: 64′ 0″ × 9′ 3″. Non-gangwayed, side doors to each seating bay
Weight: **Seats:** 2nd, 95

W56280	W56282	W56284	W56286	W56288	W56289
W56281	W56283	W56285	W56287		

Gloucester R. C. & W. Co. (2)
DRIVING TRAILER SECOND ■

(For use with Single Unit cars Nos. W55000-35)
Introduced: 1958
Body: 64′ 0″ × 9′ 3″. Non-gangwayed, side doors to each seating bay
Weight: 29 tons   **Seats:** 2nd, 95

M 56291	M 56293	M56295	W56297	W56298	M56299
W56292	W56294	M56296			

Gloucester R.C. & W. Co. driving trailer second No. W56293　　　　　[*P. H. Wells*

Gloucester R.C. & W. Co. twin unit arriving at Polmont　　　　　[*S. Rickard*

Metro-Cammell trailer brake second No. NE59093　　　　　[*D. L. Percival*

Gloucester R. C. & W. Co. (2)

DRIVING TRAILER COMPOSITE (L) ■
Introduced: 1957

For details see SC56094-M56113

SC56300	SC56303	SC56308	SC56311	SC56314	SC56317
SC56301	SC56306	SC56309	SC56312	SC56315	SC56318
SC56302	SC56307	SC56310	SC56313	SC56316	SC56319

Metropolitan-Cammell (2)

DRIVING TRAILER COMPOSITE (L) ■
Introduced: 1958

Body: 57′ 0″ × 9′ 3″   **Weight:** 25 tons   **Seats:** 1st, 12; 2nd, 53

M56332	M56346	M56360	NE56373	SC56386	SC56399
M56333	M56347	M56361	NE56374	SC56387	SC56400
M56334	M56348	NE56362	NE56375	SC56388	SC56401
M56335	M56349	NE56363	NE56376	SC56389	SC56402
M56336	M56350	NE56364	NE56377	SC56390	SC56403
M56337	M56351	NE56365	NE56378	SC56391	SC56404
M56338	M56352	NE56366	NE56379	SC56392	SC56405
M56339	M56353	NE56367	NE56380	SC56393	SC56406
M56340	M56354	NE56368	NE56381	SC56394	SC56407
M56341	M56355	NE56369	SC56382	SC56395	SC56408
M56342	M56356	NE56370	SC56383	SC56396	SC56409
M56343	M56357	NE56371	SC56384	SC56397	SC56410
M56344	M56358	NE56372	SC56385	SC56398	SC56411
M56345	M56359				

Cravens (2)

DRIVING TRAILER COMPOSITE (L) ■
Introduced: 1958

Body: 57′ 6″ × 9′ 2″   **Weight:** 24 tons   **Seats:** 1st, 12; 2nd, 51

E56412	E56424	E56436	E56448	E56460	SC56472
E56413	E56425	E56437	E56449	E56461	SC56473
E56414	E56426	E56438	E56450	SC56462	SC56474
E56415	E56427	E56439	E56451	SC56463	SC56475
E56416	E56428	E56440	E56452	SC56464	SC56476
E56417	E56429	E56441	E56453	SC56465	SC56477
E56418	E56430	E56442	E56454	SC56466	SC56478
E56419	E56431	E56443	E56455	SC56467	SC56479
E56420	E56432	E56444	E56456	SC56468	SC56480
E56421	E56433	E56445	E56457	SC56469	SC56481
E56422	E56434	E56446	E56458	SC56470	SC56482
E56423	E56435	E56447	E56459	SC56471	SC56483

Derby Works, B.R. (2)

DRIVING TRAILER COMPOSITE (L) ∎

Introduced: 1960
Body: 57′ 6″ × 9′ 2″   Weight: 22 tons   Seats: 1st, 12; 2nd, 53

M56484	M56488	M56492	M56496	M56499	M56502
M56485	M56489	M56493	M56497	M56500	M56503
M56486	M56490	M56494	M56498	M56501	M56504
M56487	M56491	M56495			

Derby Works, B.R. (3 Suburban)

TRAILER COMPOSITE ∎

Introduced: 1957
Body: 63′ 8¾″ × 9′ 3″. Non-gangwayed, side doors to each seating bay
Weight: 28 tons 10 cwt   Seats: 1st, 28; 2nd, 74

M59000	M59006	M59012	M59017	M59022	M 59027
M59001	M59007	M59013	M59018	M59023	M 59028
M59002	M59008	M59014	M59019	M59024	W59029
M59003	M59009	M59015	M59020	M59025	W59030
M59004	M 59010	M59016	M59021	M59026	W59031
M59005	M 59011				

Derby Works, B.R. (3 Suburban)

TRAILER SECOND ∎

Introduced: 1957
Body: 63′ 8¾″ × 9′ 3″. Non-gangwayed, side doors to each seating bay
Weight: 28 tons 10 cwt   Seats: 2nd, 106

W59032	W59034	W59036	W59038	W59040	W59041
W59033	W59035	W59037	W59039		

Metropolitan-Cammell (4)

TRAILER SECOND (L) ∎

Introduced: 1956
Body: 57′ 0″ × 9′ 3″   Weight: 25 tons   Seats: 2nd, 61

NE59042	NE59043	NE59045	NE59046	NE59047	NE59048

Metropolitan-Cammell (4)

TRAILER BRAKE SECOND (L) ∎

Introduced: 1956
Body: 57′ 0″ × 9′ 3″   Weight: 25 tons   Seats: 2nd, 45

NE59049	NE59051	NE59052	NE59053	NE59054	NE59055
NE59050					

Metropolitan-Cammell   (4)

TRAILER SECOND (L)   ■
Introduced: 1957

Body: 57' 0" × 9' 3"		Weight: 25 tons			Seats: 2nd, 71
NE59060	NE59063	NE59065	E59067	NE59069	NE59071
E59061	NE59064	NE59066	NE59068	NE59070	NE59072
NE59062					

Metropolitan-Cammell   (4)

TRAILER BRAKE SECOND (L)   ■
Introduced: 1957

Body: 57' 0" × 9' 3"		Weight: 25 tons			Seats: 2nd, 53
NE59073	NE59076	NE59078	E59080	NE59082	NE59084
E59074	NE59077	NE59079	NE59081	NE59083	NE59085
NE59075					

Metropolitan-Cammell   (4)

TRAILER SECOND (L)   ■
Introduced: 1957

For details see NE59042-8

NE59086   NE59087   NE59088   NE59089   NE59090   NE59091

Metropolitan-Cammell   (4)

TRAILER BRAKE SECOND (L)   ■
Introduced: 1957

For details see NE59049-55

NE59092   NE59093   NE59094   NE59095   NE59096   NE59097

Swindon Works, B.R.   (3 or 6 Inter-City)

TRAILER BUFFET FIRST (L)   ●
Introduced: 1961

Body:	Weight:	Seats: 1st, ; Buffet
SC59098	SC59099	

Metropolitan-Cammell   (3)

TRAILER SECOND (L)   ■
Introduced: 1957

Body: 57' 0" × 9' 3"		Weight: 24 tons 10 cwt			Seats: 2nd, 71
NE59100	NE59102	NE59104	NE59106	NE59108	NE59109
NE59101	NE59103	NE59105	NE59107		

Metropolitan-Cammell (4)

TRAILER BRAKE SECOND (L) ∎
Introduced: 1957
Body: 57' 0" × 9' 3"   **Weight:** 25 tons   **Seats:** 2nd, 53

NE59112 NE59113

Metropolitan-Cammell (3)

TRAILER COMPOSITE (L) ∎
Introduced: 1958
Body: 57' 0" × 9' 3"   **Weight:** 25 tons   **Seats:** 1st, 12; 2nd, 53

M59114	M59117	M59120	M59123	M59126	M59129
M59115	M59118	M59121	M59124	M59127	M59130
M59116	M59119	M59122	M59125	M59128	M59131

Birmingham R. C. & W. Co. (3)

TRAILER COMPOSITE (L) ∎
Introduced: 1957
Body: 57' 0" × 9' 3"   **Weight:** 24 tons   **Seats:** 1st, 12; 2nd, 54

M59132	M59142	M59152	M59161	M59170	M59179
M59133	M59143	M59153	M59162	M59171	M59180
M59134	M59144	M59154	M59163	M59172	M59181
M59135	M59145	M59155	M59164	M59173	M59182
M59136	M59146	M59156	M59165	M59174	M59183
M59137	M59147	M59157	M59166	M59175	M59184
M59138	M59148	M59158	M59167	M59176	M59185
M59139	M59149	M59159	M59168	M59177	M59186
M59140	M59150	M59160	M59169	M59178	M59187
M59141	M59151				

Birmingham R. C. & W. Co. (4)

TRAILER SECOND (L) ∎
Introduced: 1958
Body: 57' 0" × 9' 3"   **Weight:** 24 tons   **Seats:** 2nd, 69

NE59188	NE59192	NE59196	NE59200	NE59203	NE59206
NE59189	NE59193	NE59197	NE59201	NE59204	NE59207
NE59190	NE59194	NE59198	NE59202	NE59205	NE59208
NE59191	NE59195	NE59199			

Birmingham R. C. & W. Co. (4)

TRAILER BRAKE SECOND (L) ∎
Introduced: 1958
Body: 57' 0" × 9' 3"   **Weight:** 25 tons   **Seats:** 2nd, 51

windon trailer second No. W59237 of a 4-car inter-city unit [A. D. McIntyre

windon trailer buffet second No. Sc59682 [D. L. Percival

1etro-Cammell 8-car Pullman unit near Slough [G. J. Jefferson

NE59209	NE59213	NE59217	NE59220	NE59224	NE59227
NE59210	NE59214	NE59218	NE59221	NE59225	NE59228
NE59211	NE59215	NE59219	NE59223	NE59226	NE59229
NE59212	NE59216				

Birmingham R. C. & W. Co. (4)

TRAILER SECOND (L) ■
Introduced: 1958

For details see NE59188-59208

NE59230 NE59231 NE59232 NE59233 NE59234

Swindon Works, B.R. (4 Inter-City)

TRAILER SECOND (L) ■
Introduced: 1963
Body: 64′ 6″ × 9′ 3″   **Weight:** 39 tons   **Seats:** 2nd, 64

W59235   W59236   W59237   W59238   W59239

Birmingham R. C. & W. Co. (4)

TRAILER BRAKE SECOND (L) ■
Introduced: 1958

For details see NE59209-29

NE59240 NE59241 NE59242 NE59243 NE59244

Derby Works, B.R. (4)

TRAILER BRAKE SECOND (L) ■
Introduced: 1958
Body: 57′ 6″ × 9′ 2″   **Weight:** 22 tons 10 cwt   **Seats:** 2nd, 50

NE59245 NE59246 NE59247 NE59248 NE59249 NE59250

Swindon Works, B.R. (3 Cross Country)

TRAILER BUFFET SECOND (L) ■
Introduced: 1958
Body: 64′ 6″ × 9′ 3″ Open second with miniature buffet at one end
Weight: 31 tons   **Seats:** 2nd, 60; Buffet, 4

W59255	W59263	W59271	W59279	W59287	W59295
W59256	W59264	W59272	W59280	W59288	W59296
W59257	W59265	W59273	W59281	W59289	W59297
W59258	W59266	W59274	W59282	W59290	W59298
W59259	W59267	W59275	W59283	W59291	W59299
W59260	W59268	W59276	W59284	W59292	W59300
W59261	W59269	W59277	W59285	W59293	W59301
W59262	W59270	W59278	W59286	W59294	

Metropolitan-Cammell (3)

TRAILER SECOND (L) ■
Introduced: 1957
Body: 57′ 0″ × 9′ 3″   Weight: 25 tons   Seats: 2nd, 71

E59302   E59303   E59304

Metropolitan-Cammell (4)

TRAILER SECOND (L) ■
Introduced: 1957
Body: 57′ 0″ × 9′ 3″   Weight: 25 tons   Seats: 2nd, 71

NE59305   NE59306

Cravens (3)

TRAILER SECOND (L) ■
OR TRAILER COMPOSITE (L)*
Introduced: 1957
Body: 57′ 6″ × 9′ 2″   Weight: 23 tons   Seats: 2nd, 69 (1st, 12; 2nd, 54*)

M59307*	M59311	M59314	M59317*	M59320*	M59323
M59308	M59312	M59315	M59318*	M59321*	M59324
M59309	M59313	M59316*	M59319	M59322*	M59325
M59310*					

Derby Works, B.R. (3 Suburban)

TRAILER COMPOSITE ■
Introduced: 1957

For details see M59000-W59031

W59326	W59335	W59344	W59353	W59361	W59369
W59327	W59336	W59345	W59354	W59362	W59370
W59328	W59337	W59346	W59355	W59363	W59371
W59329	W59338	W59347	W59356	W59364	W59372
W59330	M59339	W59348	W59357	W59365	W59373
W59331	W59340	W59349	W59358	W59366	W59374
W59332	M59341	W59350	W59359	W59367	W59375
W59333	M59342	M59351	W59360	W59368	W59376
W59334	W59343	W59352			

Derby Works, B.R. (3* or 4)

TRAILER SECOND (L) ■
Introduced: 1958
Body: 57′ 6″ × 9′ 2″   Weight: 22 tons (22 tons 10 cwt*)   Seats: 2nd, 68

NE59380	NE59382	NE59384	E59386*	E59388*	E59390*
NE59381	NE59383	NE59385	E59387*	E59389*	

Swindon Works, B.R. (3 or 6 Inter-City)

TRAILER FIRST (K) ●
Introduced: 1959
Body: 64′ 6″ × 9′ 3″   **Weight:**   **Seats:** 1st, 42

SC59391	SC59393	SC59395	SC59397	SC59399	SC59400
SC59392	SC59394	SC59396	SC59398		

Swindon Works, B.R. (3 or 6 Inter-City)

TRAILER COMPOSITE (L) ●
Introduced: 1959
Body: 64′ 6″ × 9′ 3″   **Weight:**   **Seats:** 1st, 18; 2nd, 32

SC59402	SC59404	SC59406	SC59408	SC59410	SC59412
SC59403	SC59405	SC59407	SC59409	SC59411	

Gloucester R. C. & W. Co. (3 Cross Country)

TRAILER BUFFET SECOND (L) ■
Introduced: 1958
Body: 64′ 6″ × 9′ 3″. Open second with miniature buffet at one end
Weight: 31 tons 8 cwt   **Seats:** 2nd, 60; Buffet, 4

W59413	M 59418	W59422	W59426	M59430	W59434
M 59414	M 59419	W59423	W59427	M59431	M 59435
W59415	W59420	W59424	W59428	M59432	W59436
M 59416	W59421	W59425	W59429	M59433	W59437
W59417					

Derby Works, B.R. (3 Suburban)

TRAILER COMPOSITE ■
Introduced: 1958
For details see M59000-W59031

M59438	M59440	M59442	W59444	W59446	W59448
M59439	M59441	M59443	W59445	W59447	

Derby Works, B.R. (3 Suburban)

TRAILER SECOND ✻
Introduced: 1958
Body: 63′ 8¾″ × 9′ 3″. Non-gangwayed, side doors to each seating bay
Weight: 28 tons 10 cwt   **Seats:** 2nd, 110

E59449	E59453	E59457	E59460	E59463	E59466
E59450	E59454	E59458	E59461	E59464	E59467
E59451	E59455	E59459	E59462	E59465	E59468
E59452	E59456				

Birmingham R. C. & W. Co. (3 Suburban)

TRAILER COMPOSITE (L) ■
Introduced: 1960
Body: 63' 10" × 9' 3". Non-gangwayed, side doors to each seating bay
Weight: **Seats:** 1st, 24; 2nd, 50

W59469	W59472	W59475	W59478	W59480	W59482
W59470	W59473	W59476	W59479	W59481	W59483
W59471	W59474	W59477			

Pressed Steel Co. (3 Suburban)

TRAILER COMPOSITE (L) ■
Introduced: 1959
Body: 63' 10" × 9' 3". Non-gangwayed, side doors to each seating bay
Weight: 30 tons   **Seats:** 1st, 24; 2nd, 50

W59484	W59491	W59498	W59505	W59511	W59517
W59485	W59492	W59499	W59506	W59512	W59518
W59486	W59493	W59500	W59507	W59513	W59519
W59487	W59494	W59501	W59508	W59514	W59520
W59488	W59495	W59502	W59509	W59515	W59521
W59489	W59496	W59503	W59510	W59516	W59522
W59490	W59497	W59504			

Metropolitan-Cammell (3 or 4*)

TRAILER COMPOSITE (L) ■
Introduced: 1959
Body: 57' 0" × 9' 3"   **Weight:** 25 tons   **Seats:** 1st, 12; 2nd, 53

NE59523*	NE59531*	NE59540*	SC59548	SC59555	SC59562
NE59524*	NE59532*	NE59541*	SC59549	SC59556	SC59563
NE59525*	NE59533*	NE59542*	SC59550	SC59557	SC59564
NE59526*	NE59534*	W59543	SC59551	SC59558	SC59565
NE59527*	NE59535*	SC59544	SC59552	SC59559	SC59566
W59528*	NE59536*	SC59545	SC59553	SC59560	SC59567
NE59529*	W59538*	SC59546	SC59554	SC59561	SC59568
NE59530*	NE59539*	SC59547			

Metropolitan-Cammell (3)

TRAILER SECOND (L) ■
Introduced: 1959
Body: 57' 0" × 9' 3"   **Weight:** 24 tons 10 cwt   **Seats:** 2nd, 71

NE59569	NE59570	NE59571	NE59572

Metropolitan-Cammell (4)
TRAILER BUFFET SECOND (L) ■
Introduced: 1960
Body: 57' 0" × 9' 3" Open second with miniature buffet at one end
Weight: 26 tons 10 cwt   **Seats:** 2nd, 53

NE59573	NE59574	NE59575	NE59576	NE59577	NE59578

Swindon Works, B.R. (3 Cross Country)
TRAILER BUFFET SECOND (L) ■
Introduced: 1960
Body: 64' 6" × 9' 3". Open second with miniature buffet at one end
Weight: 30 tons 12 cwt   **Seats:** 60; Buffet, 4

W59579	W59581	W59583	W59585	W59587	W59588
W59580	W59582	W59584	W59586		

Derby Works, B.R. (4 Suburban)
TRAILER SECOND (L) ■
Introduced: 1959
Body: 63' 10" × 9' 3". Non-gangwayed, side doors to each seating bay. Intermediate lavatories on each side of central passageway
Weight: 30 tons   **Seats:** 2nd, 90

M59589	M59594	M59599	M59604	M59609	M59614
M59590	M59595	M59600	M59605	M59610	M59615
M59591	M59596	M59601	M59606	M59611	M59616
M59592	M59597	M59602	M59607	M59612	M59617
M59593	M59598	M59603	M59608	M59613	M59618

Derby Works, B.R. (4 Suburban)
TRAILER SECOND ■
Introduced: 1959
Body: 63' 8¾" × 9' 3". Non-gangwayed, side doors to each seating bay
Weight: 29 tons   **Seats:** 2nd, 106

M59619	M59627	M59635	M59643	M59650	M59657
M59620	M59628	M59636	M59644	M59651	M59658
M59621	M59629	M59637	M59645	M59652	M59659
M59622	M59630	M59638	M59646	M59653	M59660
M59623	M59631	M59639	M59647	M59654	M59661
M59624	M59632	M59640	M59648	M59655	M59662
M59625	M59633	M59641	M59649	M59656	M59663
M59626	M59634	M59642			

Derby Works, B.R.   (4 Suburban)

TRAILER COMPOSITE (L) ■

Introduced: 1960

Body: 63' 6" × 9' 3". Non-gangwayed, side doors to each seating bay

Weight: 30 tons   **Seats:** 1st, 30; 2nd, 40

M59664	M59667	M59670	M59673	M59675	M59677
M59665	M59668	M59671	M59674	M59676	M59678
M59666	M59669	M59672			

Swindon Works, B.R.   (3 Cross Country)

TRAILER BUFFET SECOND (L) ■

Introduced: 1959

Body: 64' 6" × 9' 3". Open second with miniature buffet at one end

Weight: 30 tons 12 cwt   **Seats:** 2nd, 60; Buffet, 4

SC59679	SC59681	SC59682	SC59683	SC59684	SC59685
SC59680					

Metropolitan-Cammell   (3)

TRAILER COMPOSITE (L) ■

Introduced: 1959

Body: 57' 0" × 9' 3"   **Weight:** 25 tons   **Seats:** 1st, 12; 2nd, 53

SC59686	SC59688	SC59689	SC59690	SC59691	SC59692
SC59687					

Birmingham R. C. & W. Co.   (3)

TRAILER SECOND (L) ■

Introduced: 1961

Body: 57' 6" × 9' 3"   **Weight:** 24 tons   **Seats:** 2nd, 72

NE59693	NE59697	NE59700	NE59703	NE59707	NE59710
NE59694	NE59698	NE59701	NE59704	NE59708	NE59711
NE59695	NE59699	NE59702	NE59705	NE59709	NE59712
NE59696					

Derby Works, B.R.   (4 Suburban)

TRAILER SECOND ■

Introduced: 1960

Body: 63' 6" × 9' 3". Non-gangwayed, side doors to each seating bay

Weight: 28 tons   **Seats:** 2nd, 106

M59713	M59714	M59715	M59716	M59717	M59718

Derby Works, B.R. (4 Suburban)
TRAILER COMPOSITE (L) ∎
Introduced: 1960
Body: 63′ 6″ × 9′ 3″. Non-gangwayed, side doors to each seating bay
Weight: 30 tons   **Seats:** 1st, 30; 2nd, 40

M59719	M59720	M59721	M59722	M59723	M59724

Derby Works, B.R. (4 Suburban)
TRAILER SECOND ∎
Introduced: 1960

For details see M59713-8

M59725	M59729	M59733	M59736	M59739	M59742
M59726	M59730	M59734	M59737	M59740	M59743
M59727	M59731	M59735	M59738	M59741	M59744
M59728	M59732				

Derby Works, B.R. (4 Suburban)
TRAILER COMPOSITE (L) ∎
Introduced: 1960

For details see M59719-24

M59745	M59749	M59753	M59756	M59759	M59762
M59746	M59750	M59754	M59757	M59760	M59763
M59747	M59751	M59755	M59758	M59761	M59764
M59748	M59752				

Swindon Works, B.R. (6 Trans-Pennine)
TRAILER SECOND (L) ∎
Introduced: 1960
Body: 64′ 6″ × 9′ 3″   **Weight:**   **Seats:** 2nd, 64

NE59765	NE59767	NE59769	NE59771	NE59772	NE59773
NE59766	NE59768	NE59770			

Swindon Works, B.R. (6 Trans-Pennine)
TRAILER BUFFET FIRST (L) ∎
Introduced: 1960
Body: 64′ 6″ × 9′ 3″   **Weight:**   **Seats:** 1st, 18; Buffet, 8

NE59774	NE59776	NE59778	NE59779	NE59780	NE59781
NE59775	NE59777				

Derby Works, B.R. (3)

TRAILER SECOND (L) ∎
Introduced: 1960

Body: 58′ 1″ × 9′ 3″   **Weight:** 28 tons   **Seats:** 2nd, 71

SC59782	SC59787	SC59792	SC59796	SC59800	SC59804
SC59783	SC59788	SC59793	SC59797	SC59801	SC59805
SC59784	SC59789	SC59794	SC59798	SC59802	SC59806
SC59785	SC59790	SC59795	SC59799	SC59803	SC59807
SC59786	SC59791				

Birmingham R. C. & W. Co. (3)

TRAILER SECOND (L) ∎
Introduced: 1961

Body: 57′ 6″ × 9′ 3″   **Weight:**   **Seats:** 2nd,

M59808	M59810	M59812	M59814	M59816	M59817
M59809	M59811	M59813	M59815		

Swindon Works, B.R. (4 Inter-City)

TRAILER COMPOSITE (K) ∎
Introduced: 1963

Body: 64′ 6″ × 9′ 3″   **Weight:** 32 tons   **Seats:** 1st, 24; 2nd, 24

W59818	W59820	W59822	W59824	W59826	W59827
W59819	W59821	W59823	W59825		

Swindon Works, B.R. (4 Inter-City)

TRAILER BUFFET SECOND ∎
Introduced: 1963

Body: 64′ 6″ × 9′ 3″   **Weight:**   **Seats:** 2nd, 32

W59828	W59829	W59830	W59831	W59832

Metropolitan-Cammell (6 Pullman Units)

MOTOR BRAKE FIRST (L)
Introduced: 1959

Engine
One North British/M.A.N. 12-cyl. pressure-charged V-type L12V18/21BS of 1,000 b.h.p.

Transmission
Electric. Two 425 h.p. G.E.C. traction motors driving through Brown-Boveri spring drive

Body: 66′ 5½″ × 9′ 3″ Guard's, luggage compartment, engine room and full width driving cab at outer end of car

Weight: 67 tons 10 cwt   **Seats:** 1st, 12

W60090	W60091	W60092	W60093

Metropolitan-Cammell (8 Pullman Units)

MOTOR BRAKE SECOND (L)
Introduced: 1959

Engine
One North British/M.A.N. 12-cyl. pressure-charged V-type L12V18/21BS of 1,000 b.h.p.

Transmission
Electric. Two 425 h.p. G.E.C. traction motors driving through Brown-Boveri spring drive

Body: 66′ 5½″ × 9′ 3″. Guard's, luggage compartment, engine room and full width driving cab at outer end of car

Weight: 67 tons 10 cwt   **Seats:** 2nd, 18

W60094	W60095	W60096	W60097	W60098	W60099

Metropolitan-Cammell (8 Pullman Units)

MOTOR PARLOUR SECOND (L)
(non-driving)

Introduced: 1959
Transmission. Electric. Two 425 h.p. G.E.C. traction motors driving through Brown-Boveri spring drive

Body: 65′ 6″ × 9′ 3″   **Weight:** 45 tons 10 cwt   **Seats:** 2nd, 42

W60644	W60645	W60646	W60647	W60648	W60649

Metropolitan-Cammell (6 Pullman Units)

MOTOR KITCHEN FIRST (L)
(non-driving)

Introduced: 1959
Transmission: Electric. Two 425 h.p. G.E.C. traction motors driving through Brown-Boveri spring drive

Body: 65′ 6″ × 9′ 3″   **Weight:** 49 tons   **Seats:** 1st, 18

W60730	W60731	W60732	W60733

Metropolitan-Cammell (8 Pullman Units)

TRAILER KITCHEN FIRST (L)
Introduced: 1959

Body: 65′ 6″ × 9′ 3″   **Weight:** 36 tons   **Seats:** 1st, 18

W60734	W60735	W60736	W60737	W60738	W60739

Metropolitan-Cammell (6 or 8* Pullman Units)

TRAILER PARLOUR FIRST (L)
Introduced: 1959

Body: 65′ 6″ × 9′ 3″   **Weight:** 33 tons   **Seats:** 1st, 36

W60740	W60742	W60744*	W60746*	W60748*	W60749*
W60741	W60743	W60745*	W60747*		

Derby Works, B.R. (2)

MOTOR BRAKE SECOND ◆

Introduced: 1954

Engines
Two B.U.T. (A.E.C.) 6-cyl. horizontal
type of 150 b.h.p.

Transmission
Mechanical. Standard

Body: 57′ 6″ × 9′ 2″ **Weight:** 27 tons **Seats:** 2nd, 61 (56*)

M79008	M79013	M79018	E79023*	E79027*	E79037*
M79009	M79014	M79019	E79024*	E79028*	E79038*
M79010	M79015	E79021*	E79025*	E79030*	E79044*
M79011	M79016	E79022*	E79026*	E79031*	E79046*
M79012	M79017				

Metropolitan-Cammell (2)

MOTOR BRAKE SECOND ◆

Introduced: 1955

Engines
Two B.U.T. (A.E.C.) 6-cyl. horizontal
type of 150 b.h.p.

Transmission
Mechanical. Standard

Body: 57′ 0″ × 9′ 3″ **Weight:** 26 tons 10 cwt **Seats:** 2nd, 57 (53*)

E79047	E79052	E79057	E79062	E79067	E79072
E79048	E79053	E79058	E79063	E79068	E79073
E79049	E79054	E79059	E79064	E79069	E79074
E79050	E79055	E79060	E79065	E79070	E79075
E79051	E79056	E79061	E79066	E79071	

Swindon Works, B.R. (3 or 6 Inter-City)

MOTOR BRAKE SECOND (L) ●

Introduced: 1956

Engines
Two B.U.T. (A.E.C.) 6-cyl. horizontal
type of 150 b.h.p.

Transmission
Mechanical. Standard

Body: 64′ 6″ × 9′ 3″. Guard's and luggage compartment at outer end. Two types of car; "leading"* with full width driving compartment, gangwayed at inner end only; "intermediate"† with side driving compartment gangwayed at both ends

Weight: 38 tons **Seats:** 2nd, 52

SC79083†	SC79088†	SC79093*	SC79098*	SC79103*	SC79108*
SC79084†	SC79089†	SC79094*	SC79099*	SC79104*	SC79109*
SC79085†	SC79090†	SC79095†	SC79100*	SC79105*	SC79110*
SC79086†	SC79091*	SC79096*	SC79101*	SC79106*	SC79111*
SC79087†	SC79092*	SC79097*	SC79102*	SC79107*	

Derby motor brake second No. E79026   *[D. L. Percival*

Swindon 6-car inter-city unit at Prestwick   *[P. J. Sharpe*

Derby driving trailer composite No. M79662   *[P. J. Sharpe*

Derby Works, B.R. (2)

MOTOR BRAKE SECOND (L) ◆

Introduced: 1955

Engines
Two B.U.T. (A.E.C.) 6-cyl. horizontal
type of 150 b.h.p.

Transmission
Mechanical. Standard
*Fitted with Self-Changing Gears Ltd.
automatic four-speed gearbox

Body: 57′ 6″ × 9′ 2″   **Weight:** 27 tons   **Seats: 2nd,** 52

M79118	M79124	M79128	M79133	E79137	M79144
M79119	M79125	M79129	M79134	E79138	M79145
M79121	M79126	M79131	M79135*	E79140	M79146
M79123	M79127	M79132	M79136	M79142	M79148

Swindon Works, B.R. (6 Inter-City)

MOTOR SECOND (L) ●

Introduced: 1957

Engines
Two B.U.T. (A.E.C.) 6-cyl. horizontal
type of 150 b.h.p.

Transmission
Mechanical. Standard

Body: 64′ 6″ × 9′ 3″. Gangwayed both ends. Side driving compartment at one end

Weight: 39 tons 3 cwt   **Seats: 2nd,** 64

SC79155	SC79158	SC79161	SC79163	SC79165	SC79167
SC79156	SC79159	SC79162	SC79164	SC79166	SC79168
SC79157	SC79160				

Derby Works, B.R. (2)

MOTOR BRAKE SECOND ◆
Introduced: 1956

For details see M79118-49

M79171	M79175	M79177	M79180	M79181

Derby Works, B.R. (2)

MOTOR BRAKE SECOND ◆
Introduced: 1956

For details see M79008-20

M79184	M79185	M79186	M79187	M79188

Derby Works, B.R. (2)
DRIVING TRAILER COMPOSITE (L) ◆
Introduced: 1955
Body: 57′ 6″ × 9′ 2″   Weight: 20 tons   Seats: 1st, 16; 2nd, 53

E79253	E79254	E79255	E79257	E79260

Metropolitan-Cammell (2)
DRIVING TRAILER SECOND (L) ◆
Introduced: 1956
Body: 57′ 0″ × 9′ 3″   Weight: 25 tons   Seats: 2nd, 71

E79263	E79268	E79273	E79278	E79283	E79288
E79264	E79269	E79274	E79279	E79284	E79289
E79265	E79270	E79275	E79280	E79285	E79290
E79266	E79271	E79276	E79281	E79286	E79291
E79267	E79272	E79277	E79282	E79287	

Swindon Works, B.R. (3 or 6 Inter-City)
TRAILER BUFFET FIRST (K) ●
Introduced: 1967
Body: 64′ 6″ × 9′ 3″. Side corridor with three first class compartments.
Buffet with kitchen, bar and saloon
Weight: 34 tons   Seats: 1st, 18; Buffet, 12

SC79440	SC79442	SC79444	SC79445	SC79446	SC79447
SC79441	SC79443				

Swindon Works, B.R. (3 or 6 Inter-City)
TRAILER FIRST (K) ●
Introduced: 1957
Body: 64′ 6″ × 9′ 3″. Side corridor with seven first class compartments and
end doors
Weight: 33 tons 9 cwt   Seats: 1st, 42

SC79470	SC79473	SC79475	SC79477	SC79479	SC79481
SC79471	SC79474	SC79476	SC79478	SC79480	SC79482
SC79472					

Derby Works, B.R. (2)
DRIVING TRAILER COMPOSITE (L) ◆

Introduced: 1954
Body: 57' 6" × 9' 2"   Weight: 21 tons   Seats: 1st, 9 (16*); 2nd, 53

M79600	M79604	M79608	M79612	E79617*	E79622*
M79601	M79605	M79609	E79613*	E79618*	E79623*
M79602	M79606	M79610	E79614*	E79619*	E79624*
M79603	M79607	M79611	E79615*	E79621*	

Metropolitan-Cammell (2)
DRIVING TRAILER COMPOSITE (L) ◆

Introduced: 1955
Body: 57' 0" × 9' 3"   Weight: 25 tons   Seats: 1st, 12; 2nd, 53

M79626	M79628	M79629	M79630	M79631	M79632
M79627					

Derby Works, B.R. (2)
DRIVING TRAILER COMPOSITE (L) ◆

Introduced: 1962
Body: 57' 6" × 9' 2"   Weight: 20 tons   Seats: 1st, 12; 2nd, 53
(converted from M79191/2/3)

M79633	M79634	M79635

Derby Works B.R. (2)
DRIVING TRAILER COMPOSITE (L) ◆
Introduced: 1955

For details see M79600-E79625

M79639	M79647	M79655	M79664	M79671	M79678
M79640	M79648	M79656	M79665	M79672	M79679
M79641	M79650	M79657	M79666	M79673	M79680
M79642	M79651	E79658*	M79667	M79674	M79681
M79643	M79652	E79660*	M79668	M79675	M79682
M79644	M79653	M79662	M79669	M79676	M79683
M79645	M79654	M79663	M79670	M79677	M79684
M79646					

Derby Works, B.R.
MOTOR BRAKE SECOND
Introduced: 1956

Engines
Two B.U.T. (A.E.C.) 6-cyl. horizontal
type of 150 b.h.p.

Transmission
Mechanical. Standard

Body: 57′ 6″ × 9′ 2″. Non-gangwayed. Driving compartments at each end

Weight: 27 tons

Seats: 2nd, 52

M79900

Park Royal Vehicles
FOUR-WHEEL RAILBUS
Introduced: 1958

Engine
B.U.T. (A.E.C.) 6-cyl. horizontal type
of 150 b.h.p.

Transmission
Mechanical. Standard. Fitted with
Self-Changing Gears Ltd. four-speed
epicyclic gearbox

Body: 42′ 0″ × 9′ 3″. Non-gangwayed

Weight: 15 tons

Seats: 2nd, 50

SC79971

A.C. Cars
FOUR-WHEEL RAILBUS
Introduced: 1958

Engine
B.U.T. (A.E.C.) 6-cyl. horizontal type
of 150 b.h.p

Transmission
Mechanical. Standard

Body: 36′ 0″ × 8′ 11″. Non-gangwayed

Weight: 11 tons

Seats: 2nd, 46

W79975   W79976   W79977   W79978

Top: Park Royal four-wheel railbus No. M79971
[*T. Rounthwaite*

Centre: A. C. Cars four-wheel railbus No. W79976
[*R. Puntis*

Right: Hastings line 6S 6-car unit No. 1006
[*P. J. Sharpe*

DEPARTMENTAL UNIT

Former numbers in brackets

D. Wickham & Co. (2)

Converted 1967 for use as General Manager's Saloon

Introduced: 1957

Engines
Two B.U.T. (Leyland) 6-cyl. horizontal type of 150 b.h.p.

Transmission
Mechanical. Standard

Body: 57' 0" × 9' 3"
   (*57' 6" × 9' 3")

Weight

DB975005 (E50416)

DB975006* (E56171)

SOUTHERN REGION DIESEL-ELECTRIC MULTIPLE-UNITS

Eastleigh Works, B.R. (6)

6 S, 6 L*† HASTINGS

(Gangwayed within set)

Introduced: 1957

MOTOR BRAKE SECOND

Engine
English Electric 4-cyl. type 4SRKT Mark II of 500 b.h.p. at 850 r.p.m.

Transmission
Electric. Two nose-suspended axle-hung traction motors

Body: 58' 0" (64' 6"*†) × 8' 2½" & 9' 0". Guard's, luggage compartment, engine room and full width driving compartment at outer end of car

Weight: 54 tons 2 cwt (55 tons*†)

Seats: 2nd, 22 (30*†)

TRAILER FIRST (K)

Body: 58′ 0″ (64′ 6″*†) × 8′ 2½″ & 9′ 0″. Side corridor with seven (eight*†) first class compartments with side door to each compartment
Weight: 30 tons (31 tons*†)   **Seats:** 1st, 42 (48*†)

TRAILER SECOND (L)

Body: 58′ 0″ (64′ 6″*†) × 8′ 2½″ & 9′ 0″
Weight: 29 tons (30 tons*†)   **Seats:** 2nd, 52 (60*†)

TRAILER SECOND (L)

Body: 58′ 0″ (64′ 6″*, 58′ 0″†) × 8′ 2½″ & 9′ 0″
Weight: 29 tons (30 tons*, 29 tons†)   **Seats:** 2nd, 52 (60*, 52†)

TRAILER SECOND (L)

Body: 58′ 0″ (64′ 6″*, 58′ 0″†) × 8′ 2½″ & 9′ 0″
Weight: 29 tons (30 tons*, 29 tons†)   **Seats:** 2nd, 52 (60*, 52†)

MOTOR BRAKE SECOND

(as above)

1001	1007	1013*	1016*	1018*	1031*
1005	1011*	1014*	1017*	1019*	1032†
1006	1012*	1015*			

Eastleigh Works, B.R.   (6)

6 B HASTINGS
(Gangwayed within set)

Introduced: 1958

MOTOR BRAKE SECOND

Engine
English Electric 4-cyl. type 4SRKT Mark II of 500 b.h.p. at 850 r.p.m.

Transmission
Electric. Two nose-suspended axle-hung traction motors

Body: 64′ 6″ × 8′ 2½″ & 9′ 0″. Guard's, luggage compartment, engine room and full-width driving compartment at outer end of car
Weight: 55 tons   **Seats:** 2nd, 30

TRAILER SECOND (L)

Body: 64′ 6″ × 8′ 2½″ & 9′ 0″ **Weight:** 30 tons   **Seats:** 2nd, 60

TRAILER BUFFET

Body: 64′ 6″ × 8′ 2½″ & 9′ 0″. Buffet with kitchen and bar; self-contained seating saloon
Weight: 35 tons   **Seats:** Buffet, 21

Hampshire 3H 3-car unit No. 1103 at Corfe Castle on a Swanage branch working

[M. P. Turvey

Reading–Redhill 3R 3-car unit No. 1204 leaving Redhill

[J. Scrace

East Sussex 3D 3-car unit No. 1310 near Honor Oak Park

[J. Scrace

174

TRAILER FIRST (K)

Body: 64′ 6″ × 8′ 2½″ & 9′ 0″. Side corridor with eight first class compartments with side door to each compartment

Weight: 31 tons   **Seats:** 1st, 48

TRAILER SECOND (L)

(as above)

MOTOR BRAKE SECOND

(as above)

1033	1034	1035	1036	1037

Eastleigh Works, B.R.   (3 or 2*)

3 H HAMPSHIRE
2 H HASTINGS*
3 H BERKSHIRE†

Introduced: 1957

MOTOR BRAKE SECOND

Engine
English Electric 4-cyl. type 4SRKT Mark II of 600 b.h.p. at 850 r.p.m.
¶Dorman type 12QTCW V-12 of 725 b.h.p.

Transmission
Electric. Two nose-suspended axle-hung traction motors

Body: 64′ 0″ × 9′ 3″. Guard's, luggage compartment, engine room and full-width driving compartment at outer end of car. Non-gangwayed, side doors to each seating bay

Weight: 56 tons   **Seats:** 2nd, 52 (42†)

TRAILER SEMI-SALOON SECOND

(three-car units only)

Body: 63′ 6″ × 9′ 3″. Non-gangwayed, side doors to each seating bay

Weight: **Seats:** 2nd, 104

DRIVING TRAILER COMPOSITE (L)

Body: 64′ 0″ × 9′ 3″. Non-gangwayed, side doors to each seating bay or compartment. 5-bay 2nd class saloon and 2 1st class compartments with intermediate lavatories, also a 2nd class compartment next to driving compartment. A luggage compartment has been fitted in place of the 2nd class compartment in the Hampshire units

Weight: 32 tons   **Seats:** 1st, 13: 2nd, 50 (62*†)

1101	1107	1113	1119*	1124	1129†¶
1102	1108	1114	1120*	1125	1130†
1103	1109	1115	1121*	1126	1131†
1104	1110	1116	1122*	1127†	1132†
1105	1111	1117	1123	1128†	1133†
1106	1112	1118			

Eastleigh Works, B.R. (3)
3 R READING-REDHILL

Introduced: 1964

MOTOR BRAKE SECOND

Engine
English Electric 4-cyl. type 4SRKT Mark II of 500 b.h.p. at 850 r.p.m.

Transmission
Electric. Two nose-suspended axle-hung traction motors

Body: 58' 0" × 8' 2½" & 9' 0". Guard's, luggage compartment, engine room and full width driving compartment at outer end of car

Weight: 54 tons 2 cwt   **Seats: 2nd, 22**

TRAILER SECOND (L)

Body: 58' 0" × 8' 2½" & 9' 0"   **Weight** 29 tons   **Seats: 2nd, 52**

B.R. Standard design

DRIVING TRAILER SECOND (SEMI-COMPARTMENT)

Body: 63' 11½" × 9' 0" & 9' 3"   **Weight:** 30 tons   **Seats: 2nd, 66**

| 1201 | 1202 | 1203 | 1204 | 1205 | 1206 |

Eastleigh Works, B.R. (3)
3 D EAST SUSSEX

Introduced: 1962

MOTOR BRAKE SECOND

Engine
English Electric 4-cyl. type 4SRKT Mark II of 600 b.h.p. at 850 r.p.m.

Transmission
Electric. Two nose-suspended axle-hung traction motors

Body: 64' 0" × 8' 6" & 9' 0". Guard's, luggage compartment, engine room and full-width driving compartment at outer end of car. Non-gangwayed, side doors to each seating bay

Weight: 56 tons   **Seats: 2nd, 42**

TRAILER COMPOSITE

Body: 63' 6" × 8' 6" & 9' 0". Non-gangwayed side doors to each seating bay or compartment. 3-bay 2nd class saloon, 4 1st class compartments, side lavatory and further 2-bay 2nd class saloon connected by side corridor.

Weight: 31 tons   **Seats: 1st, 24: 2nd, 42**

DRIVING TRAILER SEMI-SALOON SECOND

Body: 64' 0" × 9' 6" & 9' 0". Non-gangwayed, side doors to each seating bay

Weight: 32 tons   **Seats: 2nd, 76**

1301	1305	1308	1311	1314	1317
1302	1306	1309	1312	1315	1318
1303	1307	1310	1313	1316	1319
1304					

B.R. ELECTRIC LOCOMOTIVES
AND MULTIPLE-UNITS

ELECTRIC locomotives on British Railways are numbered in two series. Those built by British Railways as part of the modernisation programme carry the prefix "E" in a series ranging from E1000 for a.c. units and from E5000 for d.c. units. The first figure of the a.c. series, in addition to identifying the locomotive, also gives an indication of its horsepower—for example, E2001 for a unit in the 2,000, h.p. range and E3001 for a locomotive in the 3,000 h.p. range. Earlier locomotives built to S.R. or L.N.E.R. designs are numbered in the 20000 series.

The headings to each class show the type designation or class, principal manufacturer and wheel arrangement. Originally the type designation A or B was intended to be used to identify locomotives suited for passenger and freight haulage respectively, but subsequent experience has shown that locomotives need not be specially geared for freight working and the designation B has disappeared.

Wheel arrangements of electric (and diesel) locomotives are described by a development of the Continental notation. This calculates by axles and not by wheels, and uses letters instead of numerals to denote driving axles ("A" = 1, "B" = 2, "C" = 3, etc.) and numerals only for non-powered axles.

If all axles on a bogie or frame unit are individually powered, a suffix letter "o" is added to the descriptive letter. Thus B.R. electric locomotive No. E5001 is shown as a Bo-Bo, indicating that it has two four-wheel bogies, each axle of which has an individual traction motor.

Electric multiple-unit trains are listed Region by Region and sub-divided into areas or lines or, in the case of the S.R., into types of stock. Details of all coaches in a particular set are listed together. The dimensions are shown length and width over body and width overall. The letter (L) in the headings indicates an open vehicle fitted with toilet facilities; (K) indicates a side corridor vehicle with toilet. Unit numbers, which are painted on the front and rear of each set, are listed where used by British Railways; otherwise individual coach numbers are shown.

English Electric Type AL3 3,300 h.p. 25kV a.c. Bo-Bo No. E3029 [*P. H. Groom*

A.E.I. Type AL5 3,300 h.p. 25kV a.c. Bo-Bo No. E3071 [*P. H. Groom*

A.E.I. Type AL1 3,300 h.p. 25kV a.c. Bo-Bo No. E3096 [*M. N. Preece*

ELECTRIC LOCOMOTIVES

Metropolitan Vickers   A1A-A1A

Introduced
1958

Equipment
Four 625 h.p. Metropolitan-Vickers nose-suspended traction motors

Driving wheel diameter
3' 8"

System
25 kV. a.c. overhead
(Rebuilt from former Gas Turbine Locomotive No. 18100)

Total h.p.
2,500

Weight
109 tons 0 cwt

Maximum tractive effort
40,000 lb

E2001

TOTAL: 1

AL1   A.E.I.   Bo-Bo
(British Thomson-Houston)

Introduced
1959

Equipment
Four A.E.I. (B.T.H.) spring-borne d.c. traction motors of 847 h.p. (continuous) driving through Alsthom quill drive

Driving wheel diameter
4' 0"

System
25 kV. a.c. overhead

Total h.p.
3,300

Weight
79 tons 12 cwt

Maximum tractive effort
48,000 lb

E3001	E3005	E3009	E3012	E3015	E3018	E3021
E3002	E3006	E3010	E3013	E3016	E3019	E3022
E3003	E3007	E3011	E3014	E3017	E3020	E3023
E3004	E3008					

TOTAL: 23

AL3   English Electric   Bo-Bo

Introduced
1960

Equipment
Four English Electric spring-borne d.c. traction motors of 740 h.p. (continuous) driving through S.L.M. resilient drives

Driving wheel diameter
4' 0"

System
25 kV. a.c. overhead

Total h.p.
3,300

Weight
73 tons 0 cwt

Maximum tractive effort
40,000 lb

E3024	E3026	E3028	E3030	E3032	E3034	E3035
E3025	E3027	E3029	E3031	E3033		

TOTAL: 12

AL4   General Electric   Bo-Bo

Introduced
1960

Total h.p.
3,300

Equipment
Four G.E.C. spring-borne d.c. traction
motors of 750 h.p. (continuous),
driving through Brown-Boveri spring
drives

Weight
76 tons 10 cwt

Driving wheel diameter
4' 0"

Maximum tractive effort
50,000 lb

System
25 kV. a.c. overhead

E3036	E3038	E3040	E3042	E3043	E3044	E3045
E3037	E3039	E3041				

TOTAL: 10

AL2   A.E.I.   Bo-Bo
(Metropolitan-Vickers)

Introduced
1960

Total h.p.
3,300

Equipment
Four A.E.I. (M.V.) d.c. traction motors
of 847 h.p. (continuous) driving
through Alsthom quill drive

Weight
78 tons 8 cwt

Driving wheel diameter
4' 0"

Maximum tractive effort
48,000 lb

System
25 kV. a.c. overhead

E3046	E3048	E3050	E3052	E3053	E3054	E3055
E3047	E3049	E3051				

TOTAL: 10

AL5   British Railways   Bo-Bo

Introduced
1960

Total h.p.
3,300

Equipment
Four A.E.I. (B.T.H.) d.c. traction
motors of 847 h.p. (continuous)
driving through Alsthom quill drive

Weight
79 tons 0 cwt

Driving wheel diameter
4' 0"

Maximum tractive effort
48,000 lb

System
25 kV. a.c. overhead

E3056	E3061	E3066	E3071	E3076	E3080	E3083
E3057	E3062	E3067	E3072	E3077	E3081	E3084
E3058	E3063	E3068	E3073	E3078	E3082	E3085
E3059	E3064	E3069	E3074	E3079		
E3060	E3065	E3070	E3075			

TOTAL: 30

AL5/1   British Railways   Bo-Bo

Introduced
1962

Total h.p.
3,300

Equipment
B.T.H.

Weight
80 tons 0 cwt

Driving wheel diameter
4' 0"

Maximum tractive effort
48,000 lb

System
25 kV a.c. overhead

E3086	E3088	E3090	E3092	E3093	E3094	E3095
E3087	E3089	E3091				

TOTAL: 10

AL1   A.E.I.   Bo-Bo
(British Thomson-Houston)

Introduced
1963

Total h.p.
3,300

Equipment
Four A.E.I. (B.T.H.) spring-borne d.c. traction motors of 847 h.p. (continuous) driving through Alsthom quill drive

Weight
80 tons 0 cwt

Driving wheel diameter
4' 0"

Maximum tractive effort
60,000 lb

System
25 kV. a.c. overhead

E3096   E3097

TOTAL: 2

AL3   English Electric   Bo-Bo

Introduced
1961

Total h.p.
3,300

Equipment
Four English Electric springborne d.c. traction motors of 740 h.p. (continuous) driving through S.L.M. resilient drives

Weight
73 tons 0 cwt

Driving wheel diameter
4' 0"

Maximum tractive effort

System
25 kV. a.c. overhead

E3098   E3099

TOTAL: 2

British Railways Type AL6 3,500 h.p. 25kV a.c. Bo-Bo No. E3141

[British Railways]

AL3/I   English Electric   Bo-Bo

Introduced
1962

Equipment
As AL3. Adopted as the test loco-motive for a stepless form of supply voltage control to the traction motors, using semi-conductor recti-fiers. Equipped with rheostatic braking

Driving wheel diameter
4′ 0″

System
25 kV. a.c. overhead

Total h.p.
3,300

Weight

Maximum tractive effort

E3100

TOTAL: I

AL6   British Railways & Vulcan Foundry   Bo-Bo

Introduced
1965

Equipment
Four AE1 type 282AZ nose-suspended traction motors

Driving wheel diameter
3′ 9″

System
25 kV. a.c. overhead

Total h.p.
3,500

Weight
81 tons 2 cwt

Maximum tractive effort

E3101	E3116	E3131	E3145	E3159	E3173	E3187
E3102	E3117	E3132	E3146	E3160	E3174	E3188
E3103	E3118	E3133	E3147	E3161	E3175	E3189
E3104	E3119	E3134	E3148	E3162	E3176	E3190
E3105	E3120	E3135	E3149	E3163	E3177	E3191
E3106	E3121	E3136	E3150	E3164	E3178	E3192
E3107	E3122	E3137	E3151	E3165	E3179	E3193
E3108	E3123	E3138	E3152	E3166	E3180	E3194
E3109	E3124	E3139	E3153	E3167	E3181	E3195
E3110	E3125	E3140	E3154	E3168	E3182	E3196
E3111	E3126	E3141	E3155	E3169	E3183	E3197
E3112	E3127	E3142	E3156	E3170	E3184	E3198
E3113	E3128	E3143	E3157	E3171	E3185	E3199
E3114	E3129	E3144	E3158	E3172	E3186	E3200
E3115	E3130					

TOTAL: 100

British Railways   Bo-Bo

Introduced
1958

Equipment
Motor generator booster set and four 638 h.p. English Electric spring-borne traction motors driving through S.L.M. flexible drive

Driving wheel diameter
4′ 0″

System
750 V. d.c. 3rd rail and overhead

Total h.p.
2,552

Weight
77 tons 0 cwt

Maximum tractive effort
43,000 lb

| E5001 | E5004 | E5008 | E5010 | E5012 | E5014 | E5020 |
| E5002 | E5007 | E5009 | E5011 | E5013 | E5018 | E5022 |

TOTAL: 14

Electro-Diesel   British Railways   Bo-Bo

Introduced
1962

Equipment
English Electric 4-cyl type 4 SRKT mark II 600 b.h.p. diesel engine; four English Electric 400 h.p. traction motors. These locomotives can work either direct from a 750 V. d.c. third rail supply or, when this is not available, with the diesel generator powering the traction motors, though at reduced horsepower

Driving wheel diameter
3′ 4″

System
750 V. d.c. 3rd rail or diesel

Total h.p.
Electric 1,600
Diesel 600

Weight
73 tons 0 cwt

Maximum tractive effort
42,000 lb

E6001	E6008	E6015	E6022	E6029	E6036	E6043
E6002	E6009	E6016	E6023	E6030	E6037	E6044
E6003	E6010	E6017	E6024	E6031	E6038	E6045
E6004	E6011	E6018	E6025	E6032	E6039	E6046
E6005	E6012	E6019	E6026	E6033	E6040	E6047
E6006	E6013	E6020	E6027	E6034	E6041	E6048
E6007	E6014	E6021	E6028	E6035	E6042	E6049

TOTAL: 49

Electro-Diesel   British Railways   Bo-Bo

Introduced
1967

Equipment

Driving wheel diameter
4′ 0″

System
750 V. d.c. 3rd rail or diesel

Total h.p.
Electric 2,550

Diesel 650

Weight

Maximum tractive effort

| E6101 | E6103 | E6105 | E6107 | E6108 | E6109 | E6110 |
| E6102 | E6104 | E6106 | | | | |

TOTAL: 10

British Railways 2,552 h.p. 750V d.c. Bo-Bo No. E5004 (in blue livery) *[J. Scrace*

British Railways 1,600/600 h.p. 750V d.c. electro-diesel Bo-Bo No. E6016 (in blue livery)
[D. L. Percival

Ex-SR 1,470 h.p. 750V d.c. Co-Co No. 20001 *[Alan Williams*

CC   S.R.   Co-Co

Introduced
1941
1948*

Equipment
Motor generator booster set and six 245 h.p. English Electric nose-suspended traction motors.

Driving wheel diameter
3′ 6″

System
750 V. d.c. 3rd rail and overhead

Total h.p.
1,470

Weight
99 tons 14 cwt
104 tons 14 cwt*

Maximum tractive effort
40,000 lb
45,000 lb*

20001   20002   20003*

TOTAL: 3

EMI   L.N.E.R. & British Railways   Bo-Bo

Introduced
1941*
1950

Equipment
Four 467 h.p. Metropolitan-Vickers nose-suspended traction motors

Driving wheel diameter
4′ 2″

System
1,500 V. d.c. overhead

Total h.p.
1,868

Weight
87 tons 18 cwt

Maximum tractive effort
45,000 lb

26000*   *Tommy*

26001	26008	25015	26022	26028	26034	26040
26002	26009	26016	26023	26029	26035	26041
26003	26010	26017	26024	26030	26036	26042
26004	26011	26018	26025	26031	26037	26043
26005	26012	26019	26026	26032	26038	26044
26006	26013	26020	26027	26033	26039	26045
26007	26014	26021				

26046	*Archimedes*	26052	*Nestor*
26047	*Diomedes*	26053	*Perseus*
26048	*Hector*	26054	*Pluto*
26049	*Jason*	26055	*Prometheus*
26050	*Stentor*	26056	*Triton*
26051	*Mentor*	26057	*Ulysses*

TOTAL: 58

Nameplate of ex-LNER Class EM1 1,868 h.p. 1,500V d.c. Bo-Bo No. 26000 *Tommy*

[*D. L. Percival*

British Railways Class EM1 1,868 h.p. 1,500V d.c. Bo-Bo No. 26007

[*M. York*

British Railways Class EM2 2,490 h.p. 1,500V d.c. Co-Co No. 27001 *Ariadne*

[*J. R. Hillier*

Introduced	Total h.p.
1954	2,490

Equipment	Weight
Six 415 h.p. Metropolitan-Vickers nose-suspended traction motors	102 tons 0 cwt

Driving wheel diameter	Maximum tractive effort
4' 2"	45,000 lb

System
1,500 V. d.c. overhead

27000	Electra	27004	Juno
27001	Ariadne	27005	Minerva
27002	Aurora	27006	Pandora
27003	Diana		

TOTAL: 7

DEPARTMENTAL LOCOMOTIVE
SOUTHERN REGION
Bo   DS75

ELECTRIC MULTIPLE-UNITS
London Midland Region

SYSTEM: 630 VOLTS D.C. 3rd AND 4th RAIL

London District Three-Car Sets
B.R. Standard design

MOTOR OPEN BRAKE SECOND
Body: 57' 5" × 9' 0" & 9' 6" **Weight:** 47 tons **Seats:** 2nd, 74
Equipment: Four 185 h.p. G.E.C. traction motors

M61133	M61143	M61153	M61163	M61172	M61181
M61134	M61144	M61154	M61164	M61173	M61182
M61135	M61145	M61155	M61165	M61174	M61183
M61136	M61146	M61156	M61166	M61175	M61184
M61137	M61147	M61157	M61167	M61176	M61185
M61138	M61148	M61158	M61168	M61177	M61186
M61139	M61149	M61159	M61169	M61178	M61187
M61140	M61150	M61160	M61170	M61179	M61188
M61141	M61151	M61161	M61171	M61180	M61189
M61142	M61152	M61162			

TRAILER SECOND
Body: 57' 1" × 9' 0" & 9' 6" **Weight:** 29 tons **Seats:** 2nd, 108

M70133	M70143	M70153	M70163	M70172	M70181
M70134	M70144	M70154	M70164	M70173	M70182
M70135	M70145	M70155	M70165	M70174	M70183
M70136	M70146	M70156	M70166	M70175	M70184
M70137	M70147	M70157	M70167	M70176	M70185
M70138	M70148	M70158	M70168	M70177	M70186
M70139	M70149	M70159	M70169	M70178	M70187
M70140	M70150	M70160	M70170	M70179	M70188
M70141	M70151	M70161	M70171	M70180	M70189
M70142	M70152	M70162			

DRIVING TRAILER
OPEN BRAKE SECOND
Body: 57' 5" × 9' 0" & 9' 6" **Weight:** 30 tons **Seats:** 2nd, 74

M75133	M75143	M75153	M75163	M75172	M75181
M75134	M75144	M75154	M75164	M75173	M75182
M75135	M75145	M75155	M75165	M75174	M75183
M75136	M75146	M75156	M75166	M75175	M75184
M75137	M75147	M75157	M75167	M75176	M75185
M75138	M75148	M75158	M75168	M75177	M75186
M75139	M75149	M75159	M75169	M75178	M75187
M75140	M75150	M75160	M75170	M75179	M75188
M75141	M75151	M75161	M75171	M75180	M75189
M75142	M75152	M75162			

BR Standard LMR London District 630V d.c. 3-car set [*G. M. Kichenside*

Trailer open composite M29834M of an LMR Wirral and Mersey 630V d.c. 3-car set [*P. J. Sharpe*

Two Wirral and Mersey 630V d.c. 3-car sets at Birkenhead North [*P. J. Sharpe*

Liverpool-Southport
Two- and Three-Car Open Sets

MOTOR OPEN BRAKE SECOND

Body: 66' 6" × 9' 3" & 9' 5"   **Weight:** 41 tons   **Seats:** 2nd, 88

Equipment: Four 235 h.p. English traction motors

M28311M	M28322M	M28332M	M28342M	M28352M	M28361M
M28312M	M28323M	M28333M	M28343M	M28353M	M28362M
M28313M	M28324M	M28334M	M28344M	M28354M	M28363M
M28314M	M28325M	M28335M	M28345M	M28355M	M28364M
M28315M	M28326M	M28336M	M28347M	M28356M	M28365M
M28316M	M28327M	M28337M	M28348M	M28357M	M28366M
M28317M	M28328M	M28338M	M28349M	M28358M	M28367M
M28318M	M28329M	M28339M	M28350M	M28359M	M28368M
M28319M	M28330M	M28340M	M28351M	M28360M	M28369M
M28321M	M28331M	M28341M			

Two Liverpool–Southport 630V d.c. 3-car sets at Liverpool (Exchange)

[J. Clarke]

TRAILER OPEN SECOND

Body: 66' 6" × 9' 3" & 9' 5" **Weight:** 24 tons **Seats:** 2nd, 102

M29545M	M29554M	M29563M	M29571M	M29579M	M29587M
M29546M	M29555M	M29564M	M29572M	M29580M	M29588M
M29547M	M29556M	M29565M	M29573M	M29581M	M29589M
M29548M	M29557M	M29566M	M29574M	M29582M	M29590M
M29549M	M29558M	M29567M	M29575M	M29583M	M29591M
M29550M	M29559M	M29568M	M29576M	M29584M	M29592M
M29551M	M29560M	M29569M	M29577M	M29585M	M29593M
M29552M	M29561M	M29570M	M29578M	M29586M	M29594M
M29553M	M29562M				

TRAILER OPEN SECOND

(Built as Composite)

Body: 66' 6" × 9' 3" & 9' 5" **Weight:** 24 tons **Seats:** 2nd, 82

M29812M	M29814M	M29816M	M29818M	M29819M	M29820M
M29813M	M29815M	M29817M			

DRIVING TRAILER OPEN COMPOSITE

Body: 66' 6" × 9' 3" & 9' 5" **Weight:** 25 tons **Seats:** 1st, 53; 2nd, 25

M29866M	M29872M	M29878M	M29884M	M29890M	M29895M
M29867M	M29873M	M29879M	M29885M	M29891M	M29896M
M29868M	M29874M	M29880M	M29886M	M29892M	M29897M
M29869M	M29875M	M29881M	M29887M	M29893M	M29898M
M29870M	M29876M	M29882M	M29888M	M29894M	M29899M
M29871M	M29877M	M29883M	M29889M		

Liverpool-Southport Single Unit

B.R. Standard design

MOTOR PARCELS VAN

Body: 64' 5" × 9' 0" & 9' 3" **Weight:** 49 tons
Equipment: Four 250 h.p. English Electric traction motors

M68000

Driving trailer second of a BR Standard Manchester – Bury 1,200V d.c. 2-car set.
[*P. J. Sharpe*

Manchester – Altrincham 1,500V d.c. 3-car set at Timperley
[*N. F. W. Dyckhoff*

Two Manchester–Glossop – Hadfield 1,500V d.c. 3-car sets
[*P. J. Sharpe*

194

Wirral & Mersey
Three-Car Open Sets

MOTOR OPEN BRAKE SECOND

Body: 58′ 0″ × 8′ 8″ & 9′ 11″ **Weight:** 36 tons **Seats: 2nd, 58**
Equipment: Four 135 h.p. B.T.H. traction motors

M28371M	M28379M	M28387M	M28394M	M28677M	M28684M
M28372M	M28380M	M28388M		M28678M	M28685M
M28373M	M28381M	M28389M	M28672M	M28679M	M28686M
M28374M	M28382M	M28390M	M28673M	M28680M	M28687M
M28375M	M28383M	M28391M	M28674M	M28681M	M28688M
M28376M	M28384M	M28392M	M28675M	M28682M	M28689M
M28377M	M28385M	M28393M	M28676M	M28683M	M28690M
M28378M	M28386M				

TRAILER OPEN COMPOSITE

Body: 56′ 0″ × 8′ 8″ & 9′ 11″ **Weight:** 20 tons **Seats: 1st, 40; 2nd, 15**

M29702M	M29710M	M29718M	M29825M	M29833M	M29840M
M29703M	M29711M	M29719M	M29826M	M29834M	M29841M
M29704M	M29712M	M29720M	M29827M	M29835M	M29842M
M29705M	M29713M		M29828M	M29836M	M29843M
M29706M	M29714M	M29821M	M29829M	M29837M	M29844M
M29707M	M29715M	M29822M	M29830M	M29838M	M29845M
	M29716M	M29823M	M29831M	M29839M	M29846M
M29709M		M29824M	M29832M		

DRIVING TRAILER OPEN SECOND

Body: 58′ 0″ × 8′ 8″ & 8′ 11″ **Weight:** 21 tons **Seats: 2nd, 68**

M29131M	M29139M	M29147M	M29155M	M29276M	M29283M
M29132M	M29140M	M29148M	M29156M	M29277M	M29284M
M29133M	M29141M	M29149M		M29278M	M29285M
M29134M	M29142M	M29150M		M29279M	
M29135M	M29143M	M29151M	M29272M	M29280M	M29287M
M29136M	M29144M	M29152M	M29273M	M29281M	M29288M
M29137M	M29145M	M29153M	M29274M	M29282M	M29289M
M29138M	M29146M	M29154M	M29275M		

SYSTEM: 1,200 VOLTS D.C. SIDE CONTACT 3rd RAIL

Manchester-Bury Two-Car B.R. Sets

B.R. Standard design

MOTOR OPEN BRAKE SECOND

Body: 63′ 11½″ × 9′ 0″ & 9′ 3″   **Weight:**   **Seats: 2nd, 84**
Equipment: Two 141 h.p. English Electric traction motors

M65436	M65441	M65446	M65450	M65454	M65458
M65437	M65442	M65447	M65451	M65455	M65459
M65438	M65443	M65448	M65452	M65456	M65460
M65439	M65444	M65449	M65453	M65457	M65461
M65440	M65445				

DRIVING TRAILER SECOND

Body: 63′ 11½″ × 9′ 0″ & 9′ 3″   **Weight:**   **Seats: 2nd, 102**

M77157	M77162	M77167	M77171	M77175	M77179
M77158	M77163	M77168	M77172	M77176	M77180
M77159	M77164	M77169	M77173	M77177	M77181
M77160	M77165	M77170	M77174	M77178	M77182
M77161	M77166				

SYSTEM: 1,500 VOLTS D.C. OVERHEAD

Manchester-Altrincham
Three-Car Sets

MOTOR BRAKE SECOND

Body: 58′ 1″ × 8′ 11″ & 9′ 3″   **Weight:** 57 tons   **Seats: 2nd, 72**
Equipment: Four 330 h.p. traction motors

M28571M	M28576M	M28580M	M28584M	M28588M	M28592M
M28572M	M28577M	M28581M	M28585M	M28589M	M28593M
M28573M	M28578M	M28582M	M28586M	M28590M	M28594M
M28574M	M28579M	M28583M	M28587M	M28591M	

TRAILER COMPOSITE

Body: 57′ 1″ × 8′ 11″ & 9′ 3″   **Weight:** 30 tons   **Seats: 1st, 24; 2nd, 72**

M29396M	M29652M	M29656M	M29660M	M29665M	M29669M
	M29653M	M29657M	M29661M	M29666M	M29670M
M29650M	M29654M	M29658M	M29662M	M29667M	M29671M
M29651M	M29655M	M29659M	M29663M	M29668M	

DRIVING TRAILER SECOND

Body: 58′ 1″ × 8′ 11″ & 9′ 3″   **Weight:** 31 tons   **Seats: 2nd, 108**

M29231M	M29235M	M29239M	M29243M	M29247M	M29250M
M29232M	M29236M	M29240M	M29244M	M29248M	M29251M
M29233M	M29237M	M29241M	M29245M	M29249M	M29252M
M29234M	M29238M	M29242M	M29246M		

Manchester-Glossop-Hadfield
Three-car Open Sets

MOTOR OPEN BRAKE SECOND

Body: 60' 4½" × 9' 0" & 9' 3" **Weight:** 50 tons 12 cwt **Seats:** 2nd, 52
Equipment: Four 185 h.p. G.E.C. traction motors

M59401	M59403	M59405	M59406	M59407	M59408
M59402	M59404				

TRAILER OPEN SECOND

Body: 55' 0½" × 9' 0" & 9' 3" **Weight:** 26 tons 8 cwt **Seats:** 2nd,

M59501	M59503	M59505	M59506	M59507	M59408
M59502	M59504				

DRIVING TRAILER OPEN SECOND

Body: 55' 4½" × 9' 0" & 9' 3" **Weight:** 27 tons 9 cwt **Seats:** 2nd, 60

M59601	M59603	M59605	M59606	M59607	M59608
M59602	M59604				

AM4/1, AM4/2* and AM4/3† Four-Car Units

B.R. Standard design

DRIVING TRAILER OPEN BRAKE SECOND

Body: 64' 0⅝" × 9' 0" & 9' 3" **Weight:** 31 tons 8 cwt **Seats:** 2nd, 82

TRAILER COMPOSITE (L)

Body: 63' 6½" × 9' 0" & 9' 3" **Weight:** 31 tons 5 cwt
Seats: 1st, 19; 2nd, 60

NON-DRIVING MOTOR BRAKE SECOND (OPEN*†)

Body: 63' 6½" × 9' 0" & 9' 3" **Weight:** 53 tons 12 cwt **Seats:** 2nd, 96 (72*†)
Equipment: Four A.E.I. 207 h.p. axle-hung nose-suspended d.c. traction motors

DRIVING TRAILER OPEN SECOND (L)

Body: 64' 0⅝" × 9' 0" & 9' 3" **Weight:** 35 tons 12 cwt **Seats:** 2nd, 80

LMR Western Lines 25kV a.c. AM4/3 4-car unit No. 039 [D. L. Percive

LMR Western Lines 25kV a.c. AM10 4-car unit No. 056 [D. L. Perciv

Scottish Region Glasgow Area 25kV a.c. AM11 3-car unit No. 105 [G. M. Kichensid

001	007	013	019*	025*	031*	036†	041†
002	008	014	020*	026*	032*	037†	042†
003	009	015	021*	027*	033*	038†	043†
004	010	016*	022*	028*	034*	039†	044†
005	011	017*	023*	029*	035*	040†	045†
006	012	018*	024*	030*			

AM10 Four-Car Units

B.R. Standard design

DRIVING TRAILER SECOND
Body: 65′ 1⅜″ × 9′ 0″ & 9′ 3″   **Weight:** 36 tons 15 cwt   **Seats:** 2nd, 80

MOTOR BRAKE SECOND
Body: 65′ 4¼″ × 9′ 0″ & 9′ 3″   **Weight:** 56 tons 7 cwt   **Seats:** 2nd, 70
Equipment: Four English Electric 270 h.p. axle-hung nose-suspended d.c. traction motors

TRAILER SECOND
Body: 65′ 4¼″ × 9′ 0″ & 9′ 3″   **Weight:** 31 tons 4 cwt   **Seats:** 2nd, 100

DRIVING TRAILER COMPOSITE
Body: 65′ 1⅜″ × 9′ 0″ & 9′ 3″   **Weight:** 33 tons 16 cwt   **Seats:** 1st, 25; 2nd, 43

UNIT Nos.

046	053	060	066	072	078	084	090
047	054	061	067	073	079	085	091
048	055	062	068	074	080	086	092
049	056	063	069	075	081	087	093
050	057	064	070	076	082	088	094
051	058	065	071	077	083	089	095
052	059						

Eastern Region

SYSTEM: 25 kV. A.C. 50 CYCLES OVERHEAD

(All Eastern Region 25 kV. multiple-units are interchangeable, and may be used on all G.E. and L.T. & S. a.c. electric lines.)

AM6 Liverpool St.–Shenfield
Three-Car Open Units

Right: ER Liverpool Street – Shenfield 25kV a.c. AM6 3-car unit No. 035
[*D. L. Percival*

Centre: ER Outer suburban 25kV a.c. AM7 4-car unit No. 132
[*P. J. Sharpe*

Bottom: ER Outer suburban 25kV a.c. AM8/1 4-car unit No. 152
[*G. M. Kichenside*

MOTOR OPEN SECOND

Body: 60′ 4½″ × 9′ 0″ & 9′ 6″　　**Weight:** 50 tons 17 cwt　**Seats: 2nd, 62**
Equipment: Four 157 h.p. nose-suspended d.c. traction motors

TRAILER OPEN BRAKE SECOND

(with transformer and rectifier)

Body: 55′ 0½″ × 9′ 0″ & 9′ 6″　　**Weight:** 26 tons　　**Seats: 2nd, 46**

DRIVING TRAILER OPEN SECOND

Body: 55′ 4″ × 9′ 0″ & 9′ 6″　　**Weight:** 27 tons 10 cwt　**Seats: 2nd, 60**

UNIT Nos.

001	013	025	037	049	060	071	082
002	014	026	038	050	061	072	083
003	015	027	039	051	062	073	084
004	016	028	040	052	063	074	085
005	017	029	041	053	064	075	086
006	018	030	042	054	065	076	087
007	019	031	043	055	066	077	088
008	020	032	044	056	067	078	089
009	021	033	045	057	068	079	090
010	022	034	046	058	069	080	091
011	023	035	047	059	070	081	092
012	024	036	048				

AM7 G.E. Outer Suburban Four-Car Units

B.R. Standard design

DRIVING TRAILER BRAKE SECOND

(with transformer and rectifier)

Body: 63′ 11½″ × 9′ 0″ & 9′ 3″　　**Weight:**　　　　**Seats: 2nd, 84**

NON-DRIVING MOTOR SECOND

Body: 63′ 6″ × 9′ 0″ & 9′ 3″　　**Weight:**　　　　**Seats: 2nd, 120**
Equipment: Four G.E.C. 174 h.p. axle-hung nose-suspended d.c traction motors

TRAILER COMPOSITE (L)

Body: 63′ 6″ × 9′ 0″ & 9′ 3″　　**Weight:** 30 tons　**Seats: 1st, 19; 2nd, 60**

DRIVING TRAILER OPEN SECOND (L)

Body: 63′ 11½″ × 9′ 0″ & 9′ 3″　　**Weight:**　　　　**Seats: 2nd, 80**

101	105	109	113	117	121	125	129
102	106	110	114	118	122	126	130
103	107	111	115	119	123	127	131
104	108	112	116	120	124	128	132

AM8/1 G.E. Outer Suburban Four-Car Units

B.R. Standard design

DRIVING TRAILER SECOND

Body: 64′ 0½″ × 9′ 0″ & 9′ 3″   **Weight:** 32 tons   **Seats:** 2nd 108

TRAILER COMPOSITE (L)

Body: 63′ 6″ × 9′ 0″ & 9′ 3″   **Weight:** 31 tons   **Seats:** 1st, 19; 2nd, 60

NON-DRIVING MOTOR BRAKE SECOND

Body: 63′ 6″ × 9′ 0″ & 9′ 3″   **Weight:** 54 tons   **Seats:** 2nd, 96

Equipment: Four English Electric 200 h.p. axle-hung nose-suspended d.c. traction motors

DRIVING TRAILER OPEN SECOND (L)

Body: 64′ 0½″ × 9′ 0″ & 9′ 3″   **Weight:** 36 tons   **Seats:** 2nd, 80

133	138	142	146	150	154	158	162
134	139	143	147	151	155	159	163
135	140	144	148	152	156	160	164
136	141	145	149	153	157	161	165
137							

AM2 Fenchurch St.–Shoeburyness Four-Car Units

B.R. Standard design

DRIVING TRAILER SECOND

Body: 63′ 11½″ × 9′ 0″ & 9′ 3″   **Weight:** 32 tons   **Seats:** 2nd, 108

TRAILER COMPOSITE (L)

Body: 63′ 6″ × 9′ 0″ & 9′ 3″   **Weight:** 31 tons   **Seats:** 1st, 19; 2nd, 60

NON-DRIVING MOTOR BRAKE SECOND

Body: 63′ 6″ × 9′ 0″ & 9′ 3″   **Weight:** 56 tons 10 cwt   **Seats:** 2nd, 96
Equipment: Four 192 h.p. English Electric nose-suspended traction motors

DRIVING TRAILER OPEN SECOND (L)

Body: 63′ 11½″ × 9′ 0″ & 9′ 3″　　　**Weight:** 36 tons　　　**Seats:** 2nd, 80

UNIT Nos.

201	215	229	243	257	271	285	299
202	216	230	244	258	272	286	300
203	217	231	245	259	273	287	301
204	218	232	246	260	274	288	302
205	219	233	247	261	275	289	303
206	220	234	248	262	276	290	304
207	221	235	249	263	277	291	305
208	222	236	250	264	278	292	306
209	223	237	251	265	279	293	307
210	224	238	252	266	280	294	308
211	225	239	253	267	281	295	309
212	226	240	254	268	282	296	310
213	227	241	255	269	283	297	311
214	228	242	256	270	284	298	312

AM8/2 Fenchurch St.–Shoeburyness
Four-Car Units

B.R. Standard design

DRIVING TRAILER SECOND

Body: 63′ 11½″ × 9′ 0″ & 9′ 3″　　　**Weight:** 32 tons　　　**Seats:** 2nd, 108

TRAILER COMPOSITE (L)

Body: 63′ 6″ × 9′ 0″ & 9′ 3″　　　**Weight:** 31 tons　　　**Seats:** 1st, 19; 2nd, 60

NON-DRIVING MOTOR LUGGAGE VAN

Body: 63′ 6″ × 9′ 0″ & 9′ 3″　　　**Weight:** 51 tons 12 cwt
Equipment: Four 192 h.p. English Electric nose-suspended traction motors

DRIVING TRAILER OPEN SECOND (L)

Body: 63′ 11½″ × 9′ 0″ & 9′ 3″　　　**Weight:** 36 tons　　　**Seats:** 2nd, 80

UNIT Nos.

313	315	316	317	318	319	320	321
314							

Top: ER Fenchurch Street–Shoeburyness 25kV a.c. AM2 4-car unit No. 264

[*G. R. Mortimer*

Centre: ER Liverpool Street–Enfield and Chingford 25kV a.c. AM5/I 3-car unit No. 431

[*P. J. Sharpe*

Right: Driving trailer semi-open composite of ER Liverpool Street–Clacton 25kV a.c. AM9/3 4-car unit No. 625

[*D. L. Percival*

AM5/1 Liverpool St.–Enfield and Chingford
Three-Car Units

B.R. Standard design

DRIVING TRAILER OPEN SECOND
Body: 63′ 11½″ × 9′ 0″ & 9′ 3″   **Weight:**   **Seats:** 2nd, 94

NON-DRIVING MOTOR OPEN BRAKE
SECOND
Body: 63′ 6″ × 9′ 0″ & 9′ 3″   **Weight:**   **Seats:** 2nd, 84

Equipment: Four G.E.C. 200 h.p. axle-hung nose-suspended d.c. traction motors

DRIVING TRAILER OPEN SECOND
Body: 63′ 11½″ × 9′ 0″ & 9′ 3″   **Weight:**   **Seats:** 2nd, 94

UNIT Nos.

401	408	415	422	429	436	443	450
402	409	416	423	430	437	444	451
403	410	417	424	431	438	445	452
404	411	418	425	432	439	446	453
405	412	419	426	433	440	447	454
406	413	420	427	434	441	448	455
407	414	421	428	435	442	449	

AM5/2 G.E. Outer Suburban Four-Car Units

B.R. Standard design

DRIVING TRAILER SECOND
Body: 64′ 0½″ × 9′ 0″ & 9′ 3″   **Weight:** 32 tons   **Seats:** 2nd, 108

TRAILER COMPOSITE (L)
Body: 63′ 6″ × 9′ 0″ & 9′ 3″   **Weight:** 31 tons   **Seats:** 1st, 19; 2nd, 60

NON-DRIVING MOTOR BRAKE
SECOND
Body: 63′ 6″ × 9′ 0″ & 9′ 3″   **Weight:** 54 tons   **Seats:** 2nd, 96
Equipment: Four G.E.C. 200 h.p. axle-hung nose-suspended d.c. traction motors

DRIVING TRAILER OPEN
SECOND (L)
Body: 64′ 0½″ × 9′ 0″ & 9′3″   **Weight:** 36 tons   **Seats:** 2nd, 80

Top: Southern Region 4-VEC unit No. 044
[*British Railways*

Centre: Southern Region BR Standard 4-TC unit No. 408 (with trailer first temporarily removed)
[*A. McIntyre*

Right: Southern Region 6-TC unit No. 601
[*D. Simmonds*

501	504	507	510	512	514	516	518
502	505	508	511	513	515	517	519
503	506	509					

AM9/I Liverpool St.–Clacton and Walton

Two-Car Units

B.R. Standard design

Gangwayed throughout

MOTOR BRAKE SECOND (L)

Body: 64' 9¾" × 9' 0" & 9' 3"   **Weight:** 59 tons 6 cwt   **Seats : 2nd, 48**
Equipment: Four 282 h.p. G.E.C. traction motors

DRIVING TRAILER OPEN SECOND (L)

Body: 64' 9¾" × 9' 0" & 9' 3"   **Weight:** 39 tons II cwt   **Seats: 2nd, 60**

UNIT Nos.

| 601 | 602 | 603 | 604 | 605 | 606 | 607 | 608 |

AM9/2 Liverpool St.–Clacton and Walton

Four-Car Buffet Units

B.R. Standard design

Gangwayed throughout

DRIVING TRAILER SEMI- OPEN COMPOSITE (L)

Body: 64' 9¾" × 9' 0" & 9' 3"   **Weight:** 39 tons 7 cwt   **Seats: Ist, 18: 2nd, 32**

NON-DRIVING MOTOR BRAKE SECOND (L)

Body: 64' 6" × 9' 0" & 9' 3"   **Weight:** 56 tons 16 cwt   **Seats: 2nd, 48**
Equipment: Four 282 h.p. G.E.C. traction motors

TRAILER GRIDDLE/BUFFET CAR

Body: 64' 6" × 9' 0" & 9' 3"   **Weight:** 35 tons 16 cwt   **Seats: Buffet, 32**

DRIVING TRAILER OPEN COMPOSITE (L)

Body: 64' 9¾" × 9' 0" & 9' 3"   **Weight:** 36 tons I cwt   **Seats: Ist, 18; 2nd, 32**

UNIT Nos.

| 611 | 612 | 613 | 614 | 615 | 616 | 617 | 618 |

AM9/3 Liverpool St.–Clacton and Walton Four-Car Units

B.R. Standard design

Gangwayed throughout

DRIVING TRAILER SEMI-OPEN COMPOSITE (L)

Body: 64' 9¾" × 9' 0" & 9' 3" **Weight:** 39 tons 7 cwt **Seats:** 1st, 18; **2nd,** 32

NON-DRIVING MOTOR BRAKE SECOND (L)

Body: 64' 6" × 9' 0" & 9' 3" **Weight:** 56 tons 16 cwt **Seats: 2nd,** 48

Equipment: Four 282 h.p. G.E.C. traction motors

TRAILER OPEN SECOND (L)

Body: 64' 6" × 9' 0" & 9' 3" **Weight:** 34 tons 8 cwt **Seats: 2nd,** 64

DRIVING TRAILER SEMI-OPEN COMPOSITE (L)

Body: 64' 9¾" × 9' 0" & 9' 3" **Weight:** 36 tons 15 cwt **Seats:** 1st, 18; **2nd** ,32

UNIT Nos.

| 621 | 622 | 623 | 624 | 625 | 626 | 627 |

Scottish Region

SYSTEM: 25 kV. A.C. 50 CYCLES OVERHEAD

AM3/1, AM3/2*, AM3/3† and AM11‡
Glasgow Suburban Three-Car Units
B.R. Standard design

DRIVING TRAILER OPEN SECOND
Body: 63′ 11⅝″ × 9′ 3″ & 9′ 3″   **Weight:** 34 tons   **Seats:** 2nd, 83

NON-DRIVING MOTOR OPEN BRAKE SECOND
Body: 63′ 6¼″ × 9′ 3″ & 9′ 3″   **Weight:** 56 tons   **Seats:** 2nd, 70

Equipment: Four A.E.I. (MV) 207 h.p. axle-hung nose-suspended d.c. traction motors

‡ Four AEI 222 h.p. axle-hung nose-suspended d.c. traction motors

DRIVING TRAILER OPEN SECOND
Body: 63′ 11⅝″ × 9′ 3″ & 9′ 3″   **Weight:** 38 tons   **Seats:** 2nd, 83

UNIT Nos.

001	015	029	043	057	071†	085	098‡
002	016	030	044	058	072	086	099‡
003	017	031	045	059	073	087	100‡
004	018	032	046	060	074	088	101‡
005	019	033	047	061	075	089	102‡
006	020	034	048	062	076	090	103‡
007	021	035*	049	063	077	091	104‡
008	022	036	050	064	078	092‡	105‡
009	023	037	051	065	079	093‡	106‡
010	024	038	052	066	080	094‡	107‡
011	025	039	053	067	081	095‡	108‡
012	026	040	054	068	082	096‡	109‡
013	027	041	055	069	083	097‡	110‡
014	028	042	056	070	084		

* Fitted with Dean door gear
† Equipped with silicon rectifiers

Southern Region

The numbers of Southern Electric units have been checked to July 1967

SYSTEM: 660/750 VOLTS NOMINAL D.C. 3rd RAIL

Three-Car Trailer Units (3-TC)

B.R. Standard design
Gangwayed throughout

DRIVING TRAILER OPEN SECOND
Body: 64′ 6″ × 9′ 0″ & 9′ 3″   **Weight:**   **Seats: 2nd,** 64

TRAILER BRAKE SECOND (K)
Body: 64′ 6″ × 9′ 0″ & 9′ 3″   **Weight:**   **Seats: 2nd,** 32

DRIVING TRAILER OPEN SECOND
(As above)

301	302	303

Four-Car Trailer Units (4-TC)

B.R. Standard design
Gangwayed throughout

DRIVING TRAILER OPEN SECOND
Body: 64′ 6″ × 9′ 0″ & 9′ 3″   **Weight:**   **Seats: 2nd,** 64

TRAILER BRAKE SECOND (K)
Body: 64′ 6″ × 9′ 0″ & 9′ 3″   **Weight:**   **Seats: 2nd,** 32

TRAILER FIRST (K)
Body: 64′ 6″ × 9′ 0″ & 9′ 3″   **Weight:**   **Seats: 1st,** 42

DRIVING TRAILER OPEN SECOND
(As above)

401	405	409	413	417	421	425
402	406	410	414	418	422	426
403	407	411	415	419	423	427
404	408	412	416	420	424	428

Six-Car Trailer Unit (6-TC)

Gangwayed throughout

DRIVING TRAILER SALOON BRAKE SECOND
Body: 63′ 6″ × 9′ 0″ & 9′ 4½″   **Weight:**   **Seats:** 2nd, 52

TRAILER SECOND (K)
Body: 63′ 6″ × 9′ 0″ & 9′ 3″   **Weight:**   **Seats:** 2nd, 68

TRAILER COMPOSITE (K)
Body: 63′ 6″ × 9′ 0″ & 9′ 3″   **Weight:**   **Seats:** 1st, 30; 2nd, 24

TRAILER SECOND (K)
(As above)

TRAILER SECOND (K)
(As above)

DRIVING TRAILER SALOON BRAKE SECOND
(As above)

601

Seven-Car Trailer Unit (7-TC)

(This unit is not equipped with push-pull control gear and cannot at present be used in multiple with powered units.)

DRIVING TRAILER BRAKE SECOND (K)
Body: 62′ 6″ × 9′ 0″ & 9′ 3″   **Weight:**   **Seats:** 2nd, 56

TRAILER SECOND
Body: 62′ 0″ × 9′ 0″ & 9′ 3″   **Weight:** 28 tons   **Seats:** 2nd, 120

TRAILER SECOND
(As above)

TRAILER COMPOSITE
Body: 62′ 0″ × 9′ 0″ & 9′ 3″   **Weight:**   **Seats:** 1st, 48: 2nd, 36

TRAILER SECOND
(As above)

TRAILER SECOND
(As above)

DRIVING TRAILER COMPOSITE (K)
Body: 62′ 6″ × 9′ 0″ & 9′ 3″   **Weight:** 31 tons 5 cwt   **Seats:** 1st, 24; 2nd, 32

701

Two-Car Units (2-BIL)
MOTOR BRAKE SECOND (K)

Body: 62′ 6″ × 9′ 0″ × 9′ 3″ **Weight:** 43 tons 10 cwt **Seats: 2nd,** 52 (56*)
Equipment: Two 275 h.p. English Electric traction motors

DRIVING TRAILER COMPOSITE (K)

Body: 62′ 6″ × 9′ 0″ & 9′ 3″   **Weight:** 31 tons 5 cwt
Seats: 1st, 24; **2nd,** 32

2001*	2022	2040	2058	2076	2095	2115	2135
2002*	2023	2041		2077	2096	2116	2136
2003*	2024	2042	2060	2078	2097	2117	2137
2004*	2025	2043	2061	2079	2098	2118	2138
2005*	2026	2044	2062	2080	2099	2120	2139
2007*	2027	2045	2063	2081	2100‡	2121	2140
2008*	2028‡	2046	2064	2082	2101	2122	2141
2009*	2029	2047	2065	2083	2103	2123	2142
2010*	2030	2048	2066	2084	2104	2124	2143
2011	2031	2049	2067	2085	2106	2125	2144
2012	2032	2050	2068	2086	2107	2126	2145
2013	2033	2051	2069‡	2087	2108	2127	2146
2015	2034	2052	2070	2089	2109	2128	2147
2016	2035	2053	2071	2090	2110	2129	2148
2017	2036	2054	2072	2091	2111	2130	2149
2018	2037	2055	2073	2092	2112	2132	2150
2019	2038	2056†	2074	2093	2113	2133‡	2151
2020	2039	2057	2075	2094	2114	2134	2152
2021							

† Units 2028/56 have BIL motor coaches and 1939-type HAL trailers
‡ Units 2069, 2100 and 2133 have BIL motor coaches and post-war all-steel
    HAL trailers

Southern Region 2-BIL unit No. 2150   [*Alan Williams*

Southern Region 1939-type 2-HAL unit No. 2611   [*Alan Williams*

Southern Region post-war all-steel 2-HAL unit No. 2700   [*J. C. Haydon*

Two-Car Units (2-HAL) 1939-type

MOTOR BRAKE SECOND

Body: 62′ 6″ × 9′ 0″ & 9′ 3″   **Weight:** 44 tons   **Seats:** 2nd, 70
Equipment: Two 275 h.p. English Electric nose-suspended traction motors

DRIVING TRAILER COMPOSITE (K)

Body: 62′ 6″ × 9′ 0″ & 9′ 3″   **Weight:** 32 tons
Seats: 1st, 18 or 24; **2nd,** 40 or 32

2601	2613	2625	2636	2648	2659	2670	2682
2602	2614	2626 *	2637	2649	2660	2671	2683
2603	2615	2627	2638	2650	2661	2672	2684
2604	2616	2628	2639	2651	2662	2673	2685
2605	2617	2629	2640	2652	2663	2674	2686
2606	2618	2630	2641	2653 †	2664	2675	2687
2607	2619	2631	2642	2654	2665	2676	2688
	2620	2632	2643	2655	2666	2677	2689
2609	2621	2633	2644	2656	2667	2678	2690
2610	2622	2634	2645	2657	2668	2679	2691
2611	2623	2635	2647	2658	2669	2681	2692
2612	2624						

* Unit 2626 has a BIL trailer
† Unit 2653 has a post-war all steel HAL trailer

Two-Car Units (2-HAL) Post-war all-steel type

MOTOR BRAKE SECOND

Body: 62′ 6″ × 9′ 0″ & 9′ 3″   **Weight:** 42 tons   **Seats:** 2nd, 84
Equipment: Two 275 h.p. English Electric nose-suspended traction motors

DRIVING TRAILER COMPOSITE (K)

Body: 62′ 6″ × 9′ 0″ & 9′ 3″   **Weight:** 31 tons   **Seats:** 1st, 18; **2nd,** 40

2693	2694	2695	2696	2697	2698	2699

Two-Car Unit (2-HAL) Post-war all-steel type

MOTOR BRAKE SALOON SECOND

Body: 62′ 6″ × 9′ 0″ & 9′ 3″   **Weight:** 39 tons   **Seats:** 2nd, 82
Equipment: Two 275 h.p. English Electric nose-suspended traction motors

DRIVING TRAILER COMPOSITE (K)

Body: 62′ 6″ × 9′ 0″ & 9′ 3″   **Weight:** 31 tons   **Seats:** 1st, 24; **2nd,** 32
2700

Four-Car Units (4-LAV)

MOTOR BRAKE SECOND

Body: 62′ 6″ × 9′ 0″ & 9′ 3″ **Weight:** 41 tons (*§44 tons, †42 tons, ‡43 tons 10 cwt) **Seats: 2nd,** 70 (†96, ‡56)

Equipment: Two 275 h.p. Metropolitan-Vickers traction motors. (*†‡§Two 275 h.p. English Electric traction motors)

TRAILER COMPOSITE

Body: 62′ 0″ × 9′ 0″ & 9′ 3″   **Weight:** 28 tons
Seats: 1st, 16; **2nd,** 70   (§29 tons)

TRAILER COMPOSITE (K)
(*TRAILER SECOND)

Body: 62′ 0″ × 9′ 0″ & 9′ 3″   **Weight:** 29 tons
Seats: 1st, 30; **2nd,** 24   (*26 tons, §30 tons)
     *2nd, 120

MOTOR BRAKE SECOND
(As above)

2921	2926*	2931	2936	2940	2944	2948	2952
2922	2927	2932†	2937	2941	2945	2949	2953
2923	2928	2933	2938	2942	2946	2950	2954§
2924	2929	2934	2939	2943‡	2947	2951	2955§
2925	2930	2935					

* Unit 2926 has one 1939-type HAL motor coach and a SUB-type trailer second
† Unit 2932 has two SUB-type motor coaches
‡ Unit 2943 has one BIL motor coach
§ Units 2954/5 are formed of later, 1939-type, HAL stock

[J. H. Bird]

Southern Region BR Standard 4-REP unit No. 3003 passing Micheldever

216

Four-Car Units (4-REP)

B.R. Standard design

Gangwayed throughout

(These units work in conjunction with 4-TC trailer units and are not normally worked in multiple with other powered units)

MOTOR OPEN SECOND

Body: 64' 6" × 9' 0" & 9' 3"   **Weight:**   **Seats:** 2nd, 64
Equipment:

TRAILER BUFFET (L)

Body: 64' 6" × 9' 0" & 9' 3"   **Weight:**   **Seats:** 19

TRAILER BRAKE FIRST (K)

Body: 64' 6" × 9' 0" & 9' 3"   **Weight:**   **Seats:** 1st, 24

MOTOR OPEN SECOND

(As above)

3001	3003	3005	3007	3009	3010	3011
3002	3004	3006	3008			

Six-Car Units (6-COR)

Gangwayed within set

MOTOR SALOON BRAKE SECOND

Body: 63' 6" × 9' 0" & 9' 5"   **Weight:** 59 tons (‡57 tons)   **Seats:** 2nd, 52 (‡56)
Equipment: *‡Four 225 h.p. B.T.H. traction motors
†Four 225 h.p. English Electric traction motors

TRAILER SECOND (K)

Body: 63' 6" × 9' 0" & 9' 3"   **Weight:** 35 tons   **Seats:** 2nd, 68

TRAILER COMPOSITE (K)

Body: 63' 6" × 9' 0" & 9' 3"   **Weight:** 35 tons   **Seats:** 1st, 30; 2nd, 24

TRAILER FIRST (K)

Body: 59' 0" × 9' 0" & 9' 3"   **Weight:** 31 tons   **Seats:** 1st, 42

TRAILER SECOND (K)

(As above)

MOTOR SALOON BRAKE SECOND

(As above)

3041‡	3043*	3045†	3047†	3048*	3049*	3050*
3042*	3044*	3046*				

‡One motor coach in unit 3041 has 56 seats.

Southern Region 6-COR unit No. 3049 emerging from Penge Tunnel

[B. Stephenson]

Five-Car Pullman Units (5-BEL)

All-Pullman: Gangwayed within set

MOTOR BRAKE SECOND PULLMAN (L)

Body: 66′ 0″ × 8′ 11½″ & 8′ 11½″   **Weight:** 62 tons   **Seats:** 2nd, 48

Equipment: Four 225 h.p. B.T.H. traction motors

TRAILER SECOND PULLMAN (L)

Body: 66′ 0″ × 8′ 11½″ & 8′ 11½″   **Weight:** 39 tons   **Seats:** 2nd, 56

TRAILER KITCHEN FIRST PULLMAN (L)

Body: 66′ 0″ × 8′ 11½″ & 8′ 11½″   **Weight:** 43 tons   **Seats:** 1st, 20

TRAILER KITCHEN FIRST PULLMAN (L)

Body: 66′ 0″ × 8′ 11″ & 8′ 11½″   **Weight:** 43 tons   **Seats:** 1st, 20

MOTOR BRAKE SECOND PULLMAN (L)

(As Above)

   3051   3052   3053

Four-Car Unit (4-BUF)

Gangwayed throughout

MOTOR SALOON BRAKE SECOND

Body: 63′ 6″ × 9′ 0″ & 9′ 4½″   **Weight:** 46 tons 10 cwt   **Seats:** 2nd, 52

Equipment: Two 225 h.p. English Electric traction motors

TRAILER FIRST (K)

Body: 63′ 6″ × 9′ 0″ & 9′ 3″   **Weight:** 33 tons

Seats: 1st, 30; 1st Dining, 12

TRAILER BUFFET (L)

Body: 63′ 6″ × 9′ 0″ & 9′ 4½″   **Weight:** 35 tons   **Seats:** Buffet, 36

MOTOR SALOON BRAKE SECOND

(As above)

3072

Four-Car Units (4-BUF)

Gangwayed throughout

MOTOR SALOON BRAKE SECOND
Body: 63′ 6″ × 9′ 0″ & 9′ 4½″   **Weight:** 46 tons 10 cwt   **Seats:** 2nd, 52
Equipment: Two 225 h.p. English Electric traction motors

TRAILER COMPOSITE (K)
Body: 63′ 6″ × 9′ 0″ & 9′ 3″   **Weight:** 32 tons 12 cwt
Seats: 1st, 30; 2nd, 24

TRAILER BUFFET (L)
Body: 63′ 6″ × 9′ 0″ & 9′ 3″   **Weight:** 37 tons   **Seats:** Buffet, 26

MOTOR SALOON BRAKE SECOND
(As Above)

3073	3075	3077	3080	3082	3083	3084	3085
3074	3076	3078	3081				

Four-Car Units (4-GRI)

Gangwayed throughout

MOTOR SALOON BRAKE SECOND
Body: 63′ 6″ × 9′ 0″ & 9′ 4½″   **Weight:** 46 tons 10 cwt   **Seats:** 2nd, 52
Equipment: Two 225 h.p. English Electric traction motors

TRAILER FIRST (K)
Body: 63′ 6″ × 9′ 0″ & 9′ 3″   **Weight:** 33 tons
Seats 1st, 30 ; 1st Dining, 12

TRAILER GRIDDLE CAR
Body: 63′ 6″ × 9′ 0″ & 9′ 4½″   **Weight:** 34 tons   **Seats:** 26

MOTOR SALOON BRAKE SECOND
(As Above)

3086   3087   3088

Southern Region 4-COR unit No. 3133 (in blue livery) [Alan Williams

Trailer Griddle Car of Southern Region 4-GRI unit No. 3086 [Alan Williams

Trailer first of Southern Region 4-GRI unit No. 3088 [G. M. Kichenside

221

Four-Car Units (4-COR)

Gangwayed throughout

MOTOR SALOON BRAKE SECOND

Body: 63′ 6″ × 9′ 0″ & 9′ 4½″   **Weight:** 46 tons 10 cwt   **Seats:** 2nd, 52
Equipment: Two 225 h.p. English Electric traction motors

TRAILER SECOND (K)

Body: 63′ 6″ × 9′ 0″ & 9′ 3″   **Weight:** 32 tons 13 cwt   **Seats:** 2nd, 68

TRAILER COMPOSITE (K)

Body: 63′ 6″ × 9′ 0″ & 9′ 3″   **Weight:** 32 tons 12 cwt
Seats: 1st, 30; 2nd, 24

MOTOR SALOON BRAKE SECOND

Body: 63′ 6″ × 9′ 0″ & 9′ 4½″   **Weight:** 46 tons 10 cwt   **Seats:** 2nd, 52
Equipment: Two 225 h.p. English Electric traction motors

3101	3110	3119	3128	3137	3145	3153	3161
3102	3111	3120	3129	3138	3146	3154	3162
3103	3112	3121	3130	3139	3147	3155	3163
3104	3113	3122	3131	3140	3148	3156	3164
3105	3114	3123	3132	3141	3149	3157	3165
3106	3115	3124	3133	3142	3150	3158	3166
3107	3116	3125	3134	3143	3151	3159	3167
3108	3117	3126	3135	3144	3152	3160	3168
3109	3118	3127	3136				

Four-Car Double Deck Suburban Units (4-DD)

MOTOR BRAKE SECOND

Body: 62′ 6″ × 9′ 0″ & 9′ 3″   **Weight:** 39 tons
Seats: 2nd, Lower deck 55; Upper deck 55 (*plus* 10 tip-up)
Equipment: Two 250 h.p. English Electric traction motors

TRAILER SECOND

Body: 62′ 0″ × 9′ 0″ & 9′ 3″   **Weight:** 28 tons
Seats: 2nd, Lower deck 78; Upper deck 66 (*plus* 12 tip-up)

TRAILER SECOND

(As Above)

MOTOR BRAKE SECOND

(As above)

4001	4002

[B. Stephenson]

Southern Region "Brighton Belle" 5-BEL unit No. 3052 near Wandsworth Common

223

Four-Car Suburban Units (4-SUB)

MOTOR BRAKE SECOND

Seats: 62′ 6″ × 9′ 0″ & 9′ 3″   **Weight:** 43 tons   **Seats:** 2nd, 102

Equipment: Two 275 h.p. English Electric traction motors

TRAILER SECOND

Body: 62′ 0″ × 9′ 0″ & 9′ 3″   **Weight:** 29 tons   **Seats:** 2nd, 132

TRAILER SECOND

Body: 62′ 0″ × 9′ 0″ & 9′ 3″   **Weight:** 29 tons   **Seats:** 2nd, 120

MOTOR BRAKE SECOND

(As Above)

4101	4103	4105	4106	4107	4108	4109	4110
4102	4104						

Four-Car Suburban Units (4-SUB)

MOTOR BRAKE SECOND

Body: 62′ 6″ × 9′ 0″ & 9′ 3″   **Weight:** 43 tons   **Seats:** 2nd, 96

Equipment: Two 275 h.p. English Electric traction motors

TRAILER SECOND

Body: 62′ 0″ × 9′ 0″ & 9′ 3″   **Weight:** 28 tons   **Seats:** 2nd, 108

TRAILER SECOND

Body: 62′ 0″ × 9′ 0″ & 9′ 3″   **Weight:** 28 tons   **Seats:** 2nd, 120

MOTOR BRAKE SECOND

(As Above)

4111	4113	4114	4115	4116	4117	4118	4119
4112							

Four-Car Suburban Unit (4-SUB)

MOTOR BRAKE SECOND

Body: 62′ 6″ × 9′ 0″ & 9′ 3″   **Weight:** 43 tons   **Seats:** 2nd, 96

Equipment: Two 275 h.p. English Electric traction motors

TRAILER SECOND

Body: 62′ 0″ × 9′ 0″ & 9′ 3″   **Weight:** 28 tons   **Seats:** 2nd, 108

Southern Region 4-LAV unit No. 2951
[J. Scrace

Southern Region double-deck 4-DD unit No. 4001
[G. M. Kichenside

Southern Region 4-SUB unit No. 4114
[P. J. Sharpe

TRAILER SECOND

Body: 62′ 0″ × 9′ 0″ & 9′ 3″   **Weight:** 28 tons   **Seats: 2nd, 120**

MOTOR SALOON BRAKE SECOND

Body: 62′ 6″ × 9′ 0″ & 9′ 3″   **Weight:** 39 tons   **Seats: 2nd, 82**
Equipment: Two 250 h.p. English Electric traction motors

  4120

Four-Car Suburban Units (4-SUB)

MOTOR BRAKE SECOND (SEMI-SALOON)

Body: 62′ 6″ × 9′ 0″ & 9′ 3″   **Weight:** 43 tons   **Seats: 2nd, 84**
Equipment: Two 275 h.p. English Electric traction motors

TRAILER SECOND

Body: 62′ 0″ × 9′ 0″ & 9′ 3″   **Weight:** 28 tons   **Seats: 2nd, 108**

TRAILER SECOND (SEMI-SALOON)

Body: 62′ 0″ × 9′ 0″ & 9′ 3″   **Weight:** 28 tons   **Seats: 2nd, 106**

MOTOR BRAKE SECOND (SEMI-SALOON)

(As Above)

4121	4123	4125	4126	4127	4128	4129	4130
4122	4124						

Four-Car Suburban Units (4-SUB)

MOTOR SALOON BRAKE SECOND

Body: 62′ 6″ × 9′ 0″ & 9′ 3″   **Weight:** 39 tons   **Seats: 2nd, 82**
Equipment: Two 250 h.p. English Electric traction motors

TRAILER SECOND

Body: 62′ 0″ × 9′ 0″ & 9′ 3″   **Weight:** 28 tons   **Seats: 2nd, 120**

TRAILER SALOON SECOND

Body: 62′ 0″ × 9′ 0″ & 9′ 3″   **Weight:** 28 tons   **Seats: 2nd, 102**

MOTOR SALOON BRAKE SECOND

(As Above)

4277	4280	4283	4286	4289	4292	4295	4298
4278	4281	4284	4287	4290	4293	4296	4299
4279	4282	4285	4288	4291	4294	4297	

Four-Car Suburban Units (4-SUB)

MOTOR BRAKE SECOND

Body: 62′ 6″ × 9′ 0″ & 9′ 3″   **Weight:** 43 tons   **Seats:** 2nd, 96

Equipment: Two 275 English Electric traction motors

TRAILER SECOND

Body: 62′ 0″ × 9′ 0″ & 9′ 3″   **Weight:** 28 tons   **Seats:** 2nd, 120

TRAILER SECOND

(As Above)

MOTOR BRAKE SECOND

(As Above)

4355	4356	4357	4358	4359	4361	4362	4363

Four-Car Suburban Units (4-SUB)

MOTOR BRAKE SECOND

Body: 62′ 6″ × 9′ 0″ & 9′ 3″   **Weight:** 43 tons   **Seats:** 2nd, 96

Equipment: Two 275 h.p. English Electric traction motors

TRAILER SECOND

Body: 62′ 0″ × 9′ 0″ & 9′ 3″   **Weight:** 28 tons   **Seats:** 2nd, 108

TRAILER SECOND

Body: 62′ 0″ × 9′ 0″ & 9′ 3″   **Weight:** 28 tons   **Seats:** 2nd, 120

MOTOR BRAKE SECOND

(As Above)

4364	4366	4368	4370	4372	4374	4375	4376
4365	4367	4369	4371	4373			

Four-Car Suburban Units (4-SUB)

MOTOR SALOON BRAKE SECOND
Body: 62′ 6″ × 9′ 0″ & 9′ 3″   **Weight:** 42 tons   **Seats:** 2nd, 82
Equipment: Two 275 h.p. English Electric traction motors

TRAILER SECOND
Body: 62′ 0″ × 9′ 0″ & 9′ 3″   **Weight:** 28 tons   **Seats:** 2nd, 120

TRAILER SALOON SECOND
Body: 62′ 0″ × 9′ 0″ & 9′ 3″   **Weight:** 28 tons   **Seats:** 2nd, 102

MOTOR SALOON BRAKE SECOND
(As Above)

4378	4380	4382	4383	4384	4385	4386	4387
4379	4381						

Four-Car Suburban Units (4-SUB)

MOTOR SALOON BRAKE SECOND
Body: 62′ 6″ × 9′ 0″ & 9′ 3″   **Weight:** 39 tons   **Seats:** 2nd, 82
Equipment: Two 250 h.p. English Electric traction motors

TRAILER SECOND
Body: 62′ 0″ × 9′ 0″ & 9′ 3″   **Weight:** 28 tons   **Seats:** 2nd, 120

TRAILER SECOND
(As Above)

MOTOR SALOON BRAKE SECOND
(As Above)

4601	4602	4603	4604	4605	4606	4607

Four-Car Suburban Units (4-SUB)

MOTOR SALOON BRAKE SECOND
Body: 62′ 6″ × 9′ 0″ & 9′ 3″   **Weight:** 39 tons   **Seats:** 2nd, 82
Equipment: Two 250 h.p. English Electric traction motors

TRAILER SECOND

Body: 62′ 0″ × 9′ 0″ & 9′ 3″   **Weight:** 28 tons (27 tons*)
Seats: 2nd, 120 (108*)

TRAILER SALOON SECOND

Body: 62′ 0″ × 9′ 0″ & 9′ 3″   **Weight:** 26 tons (28 tons)   **Seats:** 2nd, 102

MOTOR SALOON BRAKE SECOND

(As Above)

4621	4638	4656	4673	4690	4707	4723*	4739*
4622	4639	4657	4674	4691	4708	4724	4740
4623	4640	4658	4675	4692	4709	4725	4741
4624	4641	4659	4676	4693	4710	4726	4742
4625	4642	4660	4677	4694	4711	4727	4743
4626	4643	4661	4678	4695	4712	4728*	4744
4627	4644	4662	4679	4696*	4713	4729	4745
4628	4645	4663	4680	4697	4714	4730	4746
4629	4646	4664	4681	4698	4715	4731	4747
4630	4647	4665	4682	4699	4716	4732	4748
4631	4648	4666	4683	4700	4717	4733*	4749
4632	4649	4667	4684	4701	4718	4734	4750
4633	4650	4668	4685	4702	4719	4735	4751
4634	4651	4669	4686	4703	4720	4736	4752
4635	4653	4670	4687	4704	4721	4737	4753
4636	4654	4671	4688*	4705	4722	4738	4754
4637	4655	4672	4689	4706			

Four-Car Suburban Units (4-EPB)

MOTOR SALOON BRAKE SECOND (‡SEMI-SALOON)

Body: 62′ 6″ × 9′ 0″ & 9′ 3″   **Weight:** 40 tons   **Seats:** 2nd, 82 (‡84)
‡63′ 11½″ × 9′ 0″ & 9′ 3″
Equipment: Two 250 h.p. English Electric traction motors

TRAILER SECOND

Body: 62′ 0″ × 9′ 0″ & 9′ 3″   **Weight:** 28 tons   **Seats:** 2nd, 120 (108*)

TRAILER SALOON SECOND (†TRAILER SECOND)

Body: 62′ 0″ × 9′ 0″ & 9′ 3″   **Weight:** 27 tons (†28 tons)
Seats: 2nd, 102 (†120)

MOTOR SALOON BRAKE SECOND

(As Above)

5001	5029	5103	5129	5156	5182	5209	5235
5002	5030	5104	5130	5157	5183	5210	5236
5003	5031	5105	5131	5158	5184	5211	5237
5004	5032	5106	5132	5159	5185	5212	5238
5005*	5033	5107	5133	5160	5186	5213	5239
5006	5034	5108	5134	5161	5187	5214	5240
5007	5035	5109	5135	5162	5188	5215	5241
5008*	5036	5110	5136	5163	5189	5216	5242
5009	5037	5111	5137	5164	5190	5217	5243
5010	5038	5112	5138	5165	5191	5218	5244
5011	5039	5113	5139	5166	5192	5219	5245†
5012	5040	5114	5140	5167	5193	5220*	5246
5013	5041	5115	5142	5168	5194	5221	5247‡
5014	5042	5116	5143	5169	5195	5222	5248
5015	5043	5117	5144	5170	5196	5223	5249
5016	5044	5118	5145	5171	5197	5224	5250
5017	5045	5119	5146	5172	5198	5225	5251
5018	5046	5120	5147	5173	5199	5226	5252
5019	5047	5121	5148	5174	5200	5227	5253
5020	5048	5122	5149	5175	5201	5228	5254
5021	5049	5123	5150	5176	5202	5229	5255
5022	5050	5124	5151	5177	5203	5230	5256
5024	5051	5125	5152	5178	5205	5231	5257
5025	5052	5126	5153	5179	5206	5232	5258
5026	5053	5127	5154	5180	5207	5233	5259
5027	5101	5128	5155	5181	5208	5234	5260
5028	5102						

*Units 5005/8, 5220 have one nine compartment trailer second.
†Unit 5245 has two trailer compartment seconds
‡Unit 5247 has one BR standard motor coach.

Four-Car Suburban Units (4-EPB)

Motor coaches only: B.R. Standard design

MOTOR SALOON BRAKE SECOND
Body: 63′ 11½″ × 9′ 0″ & 9′ 3″ **Weight:** 40 tons   **Seats:** 2nd, 84

TRAILER SECOND
Body: 62′ 0″ × 9′ 0″ & 9′ 3″   **Weight:** 28 tons   **Seats:** 2nd, 120

TRAILER SALOON SECOND (*TRAILER SECOND)
Body: 62′ 0″ × 9′ 0″ & 9′ 3″   **Weight:** 27 tons   **Seats:** 2nd, 102

MOTOR SALOON BRAKE SECOND

(As above)

5261*	5262	5301	5302

* Unit 5261 has two trailer compartment seconds

Top: Southern Region 4-EPB unit No. 5015
[B. Stephenson

Centre: Southern Region 2-EPB unit No. 5682
[Alan Williams

Right: Southern Region BR Standard 2-HAP unit No. 6165
[J. H. Bird

Four-Car Suburban Units (4-EPB)

B.R. Standard design

MOTOR SALOON BRAKE SECOND

Body: 63′ 11½″ × 9′ 0″ & 9′ 3″ **Weight:** 39 tons or 40 tons

Seats: 2nd, 82

Equipment: Two 250 h.p. English Electric traction motors

TRAILER SECOND (SEMI-COMPARTMENT)

Body: 63′ 6″ × 9′ 0″ & 9′ 3″ **Weight:** 29 tons **Seats:** 2nd, 112

TRAILER SECOND (SEMI-COMPARTMENT)

(As Above)

MOTOR SALOON BRAKE SECOND

(As Above)

5303	5312	5321	5330	5339	5347	5355	5363
5304	5313	5322	5331	5340	5348	5356	5364
5305	5314	5323	5332	5341	5349	5357	5365
5306	5315	5324	5333	5342	5350	5358	5366
5307	5316	5325	5334	5343	5351	5359	5367
5308	5317	5326	5335	5344	5352	5360	5368
5309	5318	5327	5336	5345	5353	5361	5369
5310	5319	5328	5337	5346	5354	5362	5370
5311	5320	5329	5338				

Two-Car Units (2-HAP)

MOTOR BRAKE SECOND (SEMI-SALOON)

Body: 62′ 6″ × 9′ 0″ & 9′ 3″ **Weight:** 40 tons **Seats:** 2nd, 84

Equipment: Two 250 h.p. English Electric traction motors

DRIVING TRAILER COMPOSITE (K)

Body: 62′ 6″ × 9′ 0″ & 9′ 3″ **Weight:** 32 tons **Seats:** 1st, 18; 2nd, 36

5601	5606	5611	5616	5621	5625	5629	5633
5602	5607	5612	5617	5622	5626	5630	5634
5603	5608	5613	5618	5623	5627	5631	5635
5604	5609	5614	5619	5624	5628	5632	5636
5605	5610	5615	5620				

Two-Car Suburban Units (2-EPB)

MOTOR BRAKE SECOND (SEMI-SALOON)
Body: 62′ 6″ × 9′ 0″ & 9′ 3″   **Weight:** 40 tons   **Seats: 2nd,** 84
Equipment: Two 250 h.p. English Electric traction motors

DRIVING TRAILER SECOND (SEMI-SALOON)
Body: 62′ 6″ × 9′ 0″ & 9′ 3″   **Weight:** 30 tons   **Seats: 2nd,** 94

5651	5656	5661	5665	5669	5673	5677	5681
5652	5657	5662	5666	5670	5674	5678	5682
5653	5658	5663	5667	5671	5675	5679	5683
5654	5659	5664	5668	5672	5676	5680	5684
5655	5660						

Two-Car Suburban Units (2-EPB)

B.R. Standard design

MOTOR BRAKE SECOND (SEMI-SALOON)
Body: 63′ 11½″ × 9′ 0″ & 9′ 3″   **Weight:** 40 tons   **Seats: 2nd,** 84
Equipment: Two 250 h.p. English Electric traction motors

DRIVING TRAILER SECOND (SEMI-COMPARTMENT)
Body: 63′ 11½‴ × 9′ 0″ & 9′ 3″ **Weight:** 30 tons (31 tons*) **Seats: 2nd,** 102

5702	5716	5726	5736	5745	5754	5763	5773
5703	5717	5727	5737	5746	5755	5764	5774
5705	5718	5728	5738	5747	5756	5765	5775
5706	5719	5729	5739	5748	5757	5767	5776
5707	5720	5730	5740	5749	5758	5768	5777
5710	5721	5731	5741	5750	5759	5769	5778
5712	5722	5732	5742	5751	5760	5770	5779
5713	5723	5733	5743	5752	5761	5771	
5714	5724	5734	5744	5753	5762	5772	
5715	5725	5735					

Two-Car Suburban Units (2-EPB)

B.R. Standard design

MOTOR OPEN BRAKE SECOND
Body: 63′ 11½″ × 9′ 0″ & 9′ 3″   **Weight:** 40 tons   **Seats: 2nd,** 74
Equipment: Two 250 h.p. English Electric traction motors

DRIVING TRAILER SECOND
Body: 63′ 11½″ × 9′ 0″ & 9′ 3″   **Weight:** 30 tons   **Seats: 2nd,**

5781	5783	5785	5787	5789	5791	5793	5795
5782	5784	5786	5788	5790	5792	5794	

Two-Car Units (2-HAP)

B.R. Standard design

MOTOR BRAKE SECOND (SEMI-SALOON)

Body: 63′ 11½″ × 9′ 0″ & 9′ 3″   **Weight:** 40 tons   **Seats: 2nd, 84**
Equipment: Two 250 h.p. English Electric traction motors

DRIVING TRAILER COMPOSITE (L)

Body: 63′ 11½″ × 9′ 0″ & 9′ 3″   **Weight:** 30 tons   **Seats: 1st, 19; 2nd, 50**

6001	6023	6045	6067	6089	6111	6132	6153
6002	6024	6046	6068	6090	6112	6133	6154
6003	6025	6047	6069	6091	6113	6134	6155
6004	6026	6048	6070	6092	6114	6135	6156
6005	6027	6049	6071	6093	6115	6136	6157
6006	6028	6050	6072	6094	6116	6137	6158
6007	6029	6051	6073	6095	6117	6138	6159
6008	6030	6052	6074	6096	6118	6139	6160
6009	6031	6053	6075	6097	6119	6140	6161
6010	6032	6054	6076	6098	6120	6141	6162
6011	6033	6055	6077	6099	6121	6142	6163
6012	6034	6056	6078	6100	6122	6143	6164
6013	6035	6057	6079	6101	6123	6144	6165
6014	6036	6058	6080	6102	6124	6145	6166
6015	6037	6059	6081	6103	6125	6146	6167
6016	6038	6060	6082	6104	6126	6147	6168
6017	6039	6061	6083	6105	6127	6148	6169
6018	6040	6062	6084	6106	6128	6149	6170
6019	6041	6063	6085	6107	6129	6150	6171
6020	6042	6064	6086	6108	6130	6151	6172
6021	6043	6065	6087	6109	6131	6152	6173
6022	6044	6066	6088	6110			

Four-Car Units (4-BEP)

B.R. Standard design

Gangwayed throughout

MOTOR SALOON BRAKE SECOND

Body: 64′ 6″ × 9′ 0″ & 9′ 3″   **Weight:** 41 tons (40 tons*)   **Seats: 2nd, 56**
Equipment: Two 250 h.p. English Electric traction motors

TRAILER COMPOSITE (K)

Body: 64′ 6″ × 9′ 0″ & 9′ 3″   **Weight:** 33 tons (31 tons*)
Seats: 1st, 24; 2nd, 24

TRAILER BUFFET

Body: 64′ 6″ × 9′ 0″ & 9′ 3″   **Weight:** 36 tons (35 tons*)   **Seats:** Buffet, 21

MOTOR SALOON BRAKE SECOND

(As Above)

7001*	7004	7007	7010	7013	7016	7019	7021
7002*	7005	7008	7011	7014	7017	7020	7022
7003	7006	7009	7012	7015	7018		

Four-Car Units (4-BIG)

B.R. Standard design
Gangwayed throughout

DRIVING TRAILER COMPOSITE (L)

Body: 64′ 6″ × 9′ 0″ & 9′ 3″   **Weight:**   **Seats:** 1st, 24; 2nd, 28

TRAILER MINIATURE BUFFET

Body: 64′ 6″ × 9′ 0″ & 9′ 3″   **Weight:**   **Seats:** 2nd, 40

NON-DRIVING MOTOR BRAKE SECOND

Body: 64′ 6″ × 9′ 0″ & 9′ 3″   **Weight:**   **Seats:** 2nd, 56
Equipment:

DRIVING TRAILER COMPOSITE (L)

Body: 64′ 6″ × 9′ 0″ & 9′ 8″   **Weight:**   **Seats:** 1st, 18; 2nd, 36

7031	7034	7037	7039	7041	7043	7045	7047
7032	7035	7038	7040	7042	7044	7046	7048
7033	7036						

Four-Car Units (4-CEP)

B.R. Standard design
Gangwayed throughout

MOTOR SALOON BRAKE SECOND

Body: 64′ 6″ × 9′ 0″ & 9′ 3″   **Weight:** 41 tons (40 tons*)   **Seats:** 2nd, 56
Equipment: Two 250 h.p. English Electric traction motors

TRAILER COMPOSITE (K)

Body: 64′ 6″ × 9′ 0″ & 9′ 3″   **Weight:** 33 tons (31 tons*)
Seats: 1st, 24; 2nd, 24

TRAILER SECOND (K)

Body: 64' 6" × 9' 0" & 9' 3"   **Weight:** 32 tons (31 tons*)   **Seats:** 2nd, 64

MOTOR SALOON BRAKE SECOND

(As Above)

7101*	7115	7129	7143	7157	7171	7185	7199
7102*	7116	7130	7144	7158	7172	7186	7200
7103*	7117	7131	7145	7159	7173	7187	7201
7104*	7118	7132	7146	7160	7174	7188	7202
7105	7119	7133	7147	7161	7175	7189	7203
7106	7120	7134	7148	7162	7176	7190	7204
7107	7121	7135	7149	7163	7177	7191	7205
7108	7122	7136	7150	7164	7178	7192	7206
7109	7123	7137	7151	7165	7179	7193	7207
7110	7124	7138	7152	7166	7180	7194	7208
7111	7125	7139	7153	7167	7181	7195	7209
7112	7126	7140	7154	7168	7182	7196	7210
7113	7127	7141	7155	7169	7183	7197	7211
7114	7128	7142	7156	7170	7184	7198	

Four-Car Units (4-CIG)

B.R. Standard design

Gangwayed throughout

DRIVING TRAILER COMPOSITE (L)

Body: 64' 6" × 9' 0" & 9' 3"   **Weight:**   **Seats:** 1st, 24; 2nd, 28

TRAILER OPEN SECOND

Body: 64' 6" × 9' 0" & 9' 3"   **Weight:**   **Seats:** 2nd, 72

NON-DRIVING MOTOR BRAKE SECOND

Body: 64' 6" × 9' 0" & 9' 3"   **Weight:**   **Seats:** 2nd, 56
Equipment:

DRIVING TRAILER COMPOSITE (L)

Body: 64' 6" × 9' 0" & 9' 3"   **Weight:**   **Seats:** 1st, 18; 2nd, 36

7301	7306	7311	7316	7321	7325	7329	7333
7302	7307	7312	7317	7322	7326	7330	7334
7303	7308	7313	7318	7323	7327	7331	7335
7304	7309	7314	7319	7324	7328	7332	7336
7305	7310	7315	7320				

Southern Region BR Standard 4-BEP unit No. 7008   [*P. J. Sharpe*

Southern Region BR Standard 4-BIG unit No. 7034   [*C. Symes*

Southern Region BR Standard 4-VEP unit No. 7710   [*A. McIntyre*

Four-Car Units (4-VEP)

B.R. Standard design

Gangwayed throughout

DRIVING TRAILER SEMI-OPEN COMPOSITE (K)
Body: 64′ 6″ × 9′ 0″ & 9′ 3″   Weight: Seats: 1st, 24; 2nd, 38

TRAILER OPEN SECOND
Body: 64′ 6″ × 9′ 0″ & 9′ 3″   Weight: Seats: 2nd, 98

MOTOR OPEN BRAKE SECOND
Body: 64′ 6″ × 9′ 0″ & 9′ 3″   Weight: Seats: 2nd, 58
Equipment:

DRIVING TRAILER SEMI-OPEN COMPOSITE (K)
(As above)

7701	7709	7717	7725	7733	7741	7749
7702	7710	7718	7726	7734	7742	7750
7703	7711	7719	7727	7735	7743	7751
7704	7712	7720	7728	7736	7744	7752
7705	7713	7721	7729	7737	7745	7753
7706	7714	7722	7730	7738	7746	7754
7707	7715	7723	7731	7739	7747	7755
7708	7716	7724	7732	7740	7748	

Isle of Wight Three-Car Units (3-TIS)

MOTOR OPEN BRAKE SECOND
Body: Weight: Seats: 2nd, 26

TRAILER OPEN SECOND
Body: Weight: Seats: 2nd, 42

DRIVING TRAILER OPEN SECOND
Body: Weight: Seats: 2nd, 38

031   032   033   034   035   036   037

Isle of Wight Four-Car Units (4-VEC)

MOTOR OPEN BRAKE SECOND
Body: Weight: Seats: 2nd, 26

TRAILER OPEN SECOND
Body: Weight: Seats: 2nd, 38 or 42

TRAILER OPEN SECOND
(As above)

MOTOR OPEN BRAKE SECOND
(As above)

041   042   043   044   045   046

Waterloo & City One- or Five-Car Units

(Tube size vehicles with air-operated sliding doors. Trains are formed of a single motor car or up to five-car units comprising two motor cars and three trailers)

MOTOR SALOON BRAKE SECOND
Body: 47′ 0″ × 8′ 7¾″   Weight: Seats: 2nd, 40
Equipment: Two 190 h.p. English Electric traction motors

51   53   55   57   59   61
52   54   56   58   60   62

TRAILER SALOON SECOND
Body: 47′ 0″ × 8′ 7¾″   Weight: 18 tons 14 cwt   Seats: 2nd, 52

71   74   77   80   83   85
72   75   78   81   84   86
73   76   79   82

Single Units

MOTOR LUGGAGE VAN

Body: 64′ 6″ × 9′ 0″ & 9′ 3″ **Weight:** 45 tons

Equipment: Two 250 h.p. English Electric traction motors

Note: These vehicles can work singly, hauling a limited load, or in multiple with EP-type stock. They are equipped with traction batteries for working on non-electrified quay lines at Dover and Folkestone

COACH Nos.

S68001	S68003	S68005	S68007	S68009	S68010
S68002	S68004	S68006	S68008		

Two-Car Departmental Motor De-Icing Units

Gangwayed within set

(Formed of the motor coaches from withdrawn Eastern Section 1925 4-SUB units; fitted with conductor rail scraping and spraying equipment)

MOTOR BRAKE

Body: 62′ 6″ × 8′ 6″ & 9′ 0″ **Weight:**

Equipment: Two 275 h.p. English Electric traction motors

MOTOR BRAKE

(As Above)

92	94	96	98	100	101
93	95	97	99		

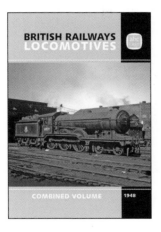

BRITISH RAILWAYS
LOCOMOTIVES

Combined Volume 1954

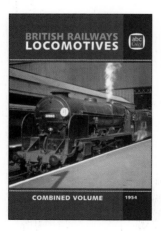

9781910809648
Price £13.50

Available from Crécy
www.crecy.co.uk

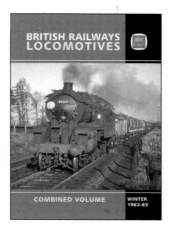

BRITISH RAILWAYS LOCOMOTIVES

Combined Volume 1964

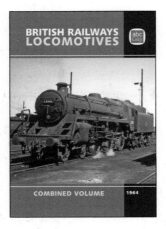

9781910809846

Price £13.50

Available from Crécy
www.crecy.co.uk